CROSSING THE AMERICAN GRAIN

ISBN 1-884532-51-9

Text set in Adobe Garamond and Meta Plus
Design and layout by Michael Buchino

Printed in Canada through Four Colour Imports, Louisville, Kentucky

Butler Books, LLC
P.O. Box 7311, Louisville, Kentucky 40207

CROSSING THE AMERICAN GRAIN

Grady Clay

BUTLER B BOOKS

I dedicate this book to my dear and loving wife, Judith McCandless.

ACKNOWLEDGEMENTS:

This is to gladly acknowledge the central contributions of my editorial associate, Hope Hollenbeck, in final editing of the book; of my wife, Judith McCandless, in organizing and providing back-up advice and judgment in all particulars; of publisher Bill Butler, who saw the prospects of a book in my assorted broadcasts; to Jerry Weston, head of WFPL, who first encouraged my entry into broadcasting, and his staff, who made broadcasting easy and the results sound better; of special friends known as "Topographic Irregulars," who have supplied a steady stream of clippings and suggestions; and finally a host of other friends and supporters through years of trial and error. Please note that any errors and omissions are mine alone, and not those of any associate.

Contents

Preface

Anyone who has kept a diary will not be surprised at the origin of these commentaries, broadcast on Public Radio WFPL, Louisville. They arise from daily encounters with the strange and the familiar in their endless presence. That constant tug-of-war between Then, Now, and Next offers plenty of stimuli for reactions that run through these commentaries.

But I should add something about their origin. Acting on advice from a wise counsel that I should record thoughts as well as travel notes, in 1962 I began keeping a form of diary in 8 x 11-inch hardback journals. (I am now on Volume 148). These have been an occasional, sometimes daily, refuge in which to record interviews, meetings, travel, and reading notes, and on occasion to summarize personal observations.

Often during the past ten years my journals also offered space in which to try out early versions of the commentaries that end up in this book. There is no single source for this continuous outpouring other than life itself. Often enough, the mere fact of writing and note taking would itself stimulate feedback—a flow of recollections or associations, which might turn out to be original observations. (Most writers know this well and learn to capture the nebulous thoughts that may emerge from routine note taking and letter writing.)

The habit of thus gathering one's thought in essay form has its roots deep in English literature, and often—as in these commentaries—is an attempt at "summing up," especially in periods of high-pressure journalism.

It happened that in the fall of 1962 I had found myself overextended with a full-time job at *The Courier-Journal* as real estate and building editor and preparing to become editor of *Landscape Architecture Magazine*, then a quarterly. In the following years I served as president of the National Association of Real Estate Editors, and of The American Society of Planning Officials (now the American Planning Association). I also found myself commuting to Washington as a member of a presidential task force on suburban problems and another to help plan the future of the Potomac River.

On one of those trips, I was occupying the jump seat in a crowded plane when all my papers spilled off the tiny table onto the floor, forcing me to take a new look at my helter-skelter paper life and resolve to better organize it. Thus began forty-odd years of journal keeping.

In retrospect, keeping a journal was also my personal reaction against the time-honored practice among newspaper reporters of using folded-up sheets of copy paper—made from newsprint—for note taking. That had always struck me as sloppy and messy, recalling the old "Front Page" movie showing pushing and shoving reporters frantically scribbling on fluttering sheets—and was long before hand-held tape-recorders had greatly altered reporting.

Out of all this flow, it seemed that some of it could take shape in more than one medium, which turned out to include this one. I wrote most of these essays in the early 1990s on the day before recording them for broadcast.

Introduction

Growing up in Atlanta, I was taught that it was, indeed, the center of the universe. Peachtree Street was for sure the model for all main drags.

Living in Cambridge, Massachusetts, taught me to be tolerant of our big neighbor Boston, the hub of the universe.

Living in Alaska I learned I was in a special place called "outside"…a long way from stateside.

Curiosity about places, those specific, generic, evanescent oddities, descended upon me early on.

Everybody I knew then believed that the way for Easterners to see—and even, with luck, to understand—the United States was to take a trip Out West. That trip spelled destiny. To travel the route of the pioneers was to go with the flow of history. The Westerners I knew had said, "To hell with the East," and wanted little to do with it.

But here I was in mid-America, the heartland with a southern beat, in a border state—"mid-western with a southern exposure," as somebody said about Louisville, Kentucky. My travels as a journalist turned the way west on its side. The cardinal points of my compass were North-South, across the American grain. I ran against the current, zigzagging, tacking to catch the winds of change. I found it a useful way to look at the world.

On the other hand, going with the flow encourages you to see what everybody else sees—same depth of focus, same foreground, same background. Sameness. That's the way to monotony, an early shape of death.

So I concluded to catch the future, let the longitudes go hang. Go with latitude and take plenty of it. North with the spring, south with the fall, or vice versa. It's time for you to tune the seasons to your pitch and your tone.

—Grady Clay, Louisville, Kentucky, August 2003

Wordplay 1

City Talk

Most of us live in and around cities, depend upon cities, and debate about making them more livable. And yet we talk about cities, using language more suited to competition than to cooperation, to controversy rather than to livability.

Consider expressions of combat and contention—how they penetrate everyday talk, and not just about city life. We "hold the line" on expenses, make a guess by "taking a cut at it," try something new by "taking a whack at it," speak of a precinct that votes the other way as "enemy territory." For a sales campaign, we "go on the warpath."

As a form of civilizing life, a city depends on civil language, the kind of talk that makes it possible to live, move, work, and negotiate in public among folks we may not know and do not control.

So…city people have to learn a special language, widely shared, called "civil discourse." I call it "survival talk."

It's lively, expressive, public talk—often loud, outgoing, easy to understand. Sometimes it's so simple it takes your breath away without sticking in your throat.

The language of cities has to be roomy and open up possibilities. It should offer space for various interpretations. It keeps the discussion open-ended. It does not shut the door, cut people off.

Its currency is "maybe so" and "let's take another look" and "on the other hand" and "have you thought about…?" It stays away from "no way!" "up yours!" and "watch where you're going, feller!" It's long on "excuse me."

This is no namby-pamby, childish chatter. It avoids gunshot. It saves lives. It gets millions of crowded, impatient people through the busy day, alive, uninjured, and in a productive frame of mind. And well on the way toward producing a livable city.

What's A Metaphor?

If you've been paying attention to the flow of new slang expressions, to changing shades of meaning, and to the language of place, stick with me for a roller coaster ride through the NEW WAVE. Not so much the words themselves, but new meanings, new usage. That's what to listen to and for.

These are metaphors, words that meant one thing when and where they got started. But you and I keep giving them new jobs to do, new workplaces. Most of them started outdoors. Now they do indoor jobs. Hang on for the FAST TURNS.

THE ADDRESS is not just your house street number, but a location in a computer's memory. You say, "GIMME A BALLPARK FIGURE." But if it's too high, you say "it's NOT IN THE BALLPARK." You establish A BEACHHEAD in somebody else's sales territory. The Supreme Court makes a BENCHMARK decision. The newspaper copy editors sit in the BULLPEN. In the restaurant there's a CARVING STATION for the roast beef.

You say "IT'S COLD OUT THERE" and you're talking job competition, not that it's freezing outdoors. If your friend CRASHED AND BURNED, he could have gone bankrupt (or gotten a divorce), but not necessarily in an aircraft crash. Gone DOWN SOUTH doesn't necessarily mean to Florida, but inattentiveness (as in OUT TO LUNCH), while "taking a FALLBACK POSITION" has moved from military to football to financial maneuvering (that is, "I'm taking a FALLBACK POSITION in such and such a stock.")

And that's only the TIP OF THE ICEBERG.

Moving Indoors

It's forever, it's for free, it's for everybody to use when they play fast and loose with the language. Everybody does it—making one word do double or triple duty, off HOME BASE. And that HOME BASE that I just took an easy slide into was...a metaphor.

We're forever taking good outdoor words and converting them to indoor usage. Let's consider LAST DITCH. It's no longer just that final, fiercely dangerous defensive position desperately taken up in combat. It can be, in today's language, a closing argument in a lawsuit; a desperate maneuver in negotiation; or, you might say, THE LAST STRAW—and that's an another outdoor metaphor that we've shifted from the farm to the indoors.

Listen to HIGH DITCH...a technical term right out of the American West and irrigation, sometimes called "THE MOTHER DITCH." But now HIGH DITCH SHOPPING means paying top dollar for merchandise in high-fashion surroundings.

But if that's too high altitude for you, come on back to HOME TERRITORY, which for most people suggests DOWN HOME, BACK HOME, AT HOME, HOME SWEET or otherwise. But when it comes tripping off tongues these days, HOME TERRITORY can mean a familiar subject, private parts of the human body, or a computer tactic that gets you back to—where else—HOME.

Meanwhile, poking its way up into everyday conversation is that ominous telltale, THE TIP OF THE ICEBERG. It's a chilling device, hinting at horrid disclosures to come...a tactical ploy suggesting that you are in touch with the invisible, in tune with the inscrutable, O! You of Great Wisdom, a person with clout, your head in the clouds, your feet among clods!

Body Snatchers

When you say, "BABY, IT'S COLD OUTSIDE" you may be talking not weather, but divorce. When you say, "IT'S A JUNGLE OUT THERE," you could be talking about a double cross in business, and not the Amazon Basin.

What would happen to conversation if words had beepers that beeped every time we body snatched a word out of its original context? What would we do for expression if words insisted on staying on their home grounds, back where they were born and raised, mostly in the Great Outdoors?

I've been tracking outdoor words as they sneak away from fresh air and wind up indoors, some kicking and screaming, some quietly. But they all are transformed…they turn into metaphors.

Eavesdrop on everyday conversations or read the papers and you're plunged "BETWEEN A ROCK AND A HARD PLACE." Not out there, but right here, indoors. A headline tells us "Lexington firm is negotiating a legal QUAGMIRE"—and all the time, you and I thought quagmires were bona fide, outdoor types of places! A novelist turns out a best-selling book, and folks say, "she HIT PAY DIRT"—a long way, she was, from the actual gold mines. Look at what happened to THE TIP OF THE ICEBURG—it's migrated south to describe situations far, far from the Arctic Circle.

And now, coming into the HOME STRETCH, headed for the FINISH LINE, I'll have to watch my step lest I CRASH AND BURN. In the *Los Angeles Times*, a columnist tells us "The American language has become a MINE FIELD in which a misstep can cost you your reputation, if not your livelihood." As I said before, speaking in metaphors, "IT'S A JUNGLE OUT THERE!"

Metaphorically Speaking

Join me for another trip through The Land of Metaphoria where the English language changes color and shape, right on the tip of our tongues.

Metaphors are words we work overtime, words we yank out of context. Hang on for some fast turns of phrase, good old outdoor words we put to new uses indoors.

FAST TURN used to be something you did on a racetrack or behind the wheel of a car. Now it's a card trick, a sexual transaction, a business maneuver, or a quick shift in conversation.

FAST TRACK has moved indoors to become an advanced curriculum for bright youngsters in school or an advanced construction schedule.

The FINISH LINE can be an indoor game or a contract deadline. If you ask, "WHO'S ON FIRST?" you may not be talking baseball, but sex—that is, who's winning at the dating game or in other competition?

If you've got a FOOTHOLD, that's not to say you're an expert mountain climber. It can suggest a pushy, intrusive, give-you-an-inch-you'll-take-a-mile sort of person.

And, look you, at FRONTLINE: once it was straight out of COMBAT ZONE (before THAT turned into the name of a honky-tonk porno district). Today FRONTLINE looks like a television tussle among showoffs.

Consider LAST DITCH...no longer that final, dangerous defense position in combat. For in today's language, it can be a closing argument in a lawsuit; a desperate maneuver in negotiation; or, you might say, the LAST STRAW. And THAT's moved indoors too.

Long ago, GUNSHOT moved off the main drag, out of the woods, and into the house—where there's far too much point-blank shooting going on.

If you thought the HOME STRETCH was the last lap of a horse-race, so it was. But in The Land of Metaphoria, it's the final, just before the end of any long, drawn-out human activity: a job, a negotiation, or even a party.

Away

Whether we're just back from, or recovering from, or looking forward to vacation, surely somewhere in all those comings and goings there occurred the magical phrase "AWAY from it all."

Many people think getting AWAY from it all is the real reason for vacations, for travel to far-off places, and to that omni-directional destination called a "GETAWAY PLACE." In getting AWAY we aim to make tracks, turn our backs, get our kicks on Route 66.

But when we talk not just about getting AWAY but about putting it AWAY, laying it AWAY, throwing it AWAY, then we're into another ballgame. Throwing things AWAY no longer works like it used to. Nor does that place called "AWAY."

The thing about AWAY is it's no longer there, waiting for whatever we want to throw AWAY. Something new gets in the way. AWAY now has overtones, undertones, legal protection. It's no longer woebegone, standing alone...it arouses neighborly objection. My throwaway falls into the public's right-of-way or my neighbor's backyard.

So here we are, surrounded by biologist Barry Commoner's Second Law of Ecology which says, "everything must go somewhere," which I translate to say "nothing ever goes AWAY."

My trash turns into your air pollution. My pile of leaves disperses into that neighborly jurisdiction called "downwind." My ashes have to go someplace—but in New York City, ash disposal sites "cost...up to $1 million an acre and often draw strong opposition."[1]

AWAY turns out to be a waif and a stray, a leftover luxury from yesterday. Just think of AWAY as somebody else's backyard, and you get the new hang of it. Don't get hung-up with it.

1: Kirk Johnson, "Why the Garbage is Never Really Gone," *New York Times*, Feb 12, 1999.

Off

This is going to be an OFF-again, on-again exploration of the place called "OFF." I will try not to go OFF limits, or OFF color, or lay OFF on you my own OFF-brand sense of humor. For I would be in danger of, as we say, putting you OFF, at which point you'd be quite correct in saying, "you're OFF-base," or "get OFF my back!" Or "Get OFF my case." Or perhaps, "Grady Clay's OFF his rocker."

I started OFF this little venture OFF the top of my head and into the OFFing by assuming that OFF is a well-known place. But like other well-known places, it monkeys around OFF duty. It may run OFF to the South Seas or OFF with somebody else's husband or wife—that is, OFF the deep end, and not necessarily in the OFF season! It was just their OFF year, you might say.

But look at what happened to them after takeOFF: the runaway couple stops at an OFF-hours bar, runs into an OFF-duty policeman who's OFF his feed, running OFF at the mouth, getting OFF a few wisecracks. "You're OFFsides," says the man.

"And you're OFFbase," says the cop.

Things go from bad to worse, and eventually they're taken OFF to jail, the man shouting, "Get OFF my back!" By this time it's clear: the runaway couple is OFF to a bad start.

They were headed, of course, for those romantic OFF islands that lie OFFshore, far OFF the beaten path, and that offer OFF-season rates for runaway couples and concupiscent others who find themselves OFF the reservation. The fact that the lady in question is wearing an OFF-the-shoulder dress complicates matters in the wee OFF-hours.... But that's another story.

Spots

There are some places we just don't quite know how to handle. We dismiss or praise them and call them "SPOTS," such as PICNIC SPOT, CHOICE SPOT, FISHING (but not HUNTING) SPOT, VACATION SPOT, FAVORITE SPOT, MAGIC SPOT, or HOT SPOT, DANGER SPOT, TROUBLE SPOT.

When we SPOT and pick a SPOT, we assert ownership, or at least possessiveness. And when we murmur, "a nice SPOT but you wouldn't want to live there!" that's faint praise indeed.

If we use American English, as most of us do, we pay tribute to food or drink by asserting "That really hits THE SPOT"—located somewhat precisely in the stomach. But to be PUT ON THE SPOT is to be put in harm's way. Remember the old gangster movies? To be PUT ON THE SPOT was to be marked for gang-style execution.

THE SPOT is a concentration zone for packing runaway energy and other loose articles. When you put SPOT to work as a verb, it means that you, with your acute vision, have SPOTTED something not easily seen by nonobservant others.

But soon enough, your family's favorite PICNIC SPOT will be discovered by unwelcome others. So into every PRIVATE SPOT, some stranger's foot may fall.

Picking the RIGHT SPOT is a venerable science in China, where they practice the ancient art of feng shui. Yet another niche is filled by THE SPOT, dating back to 1861 when the expression "to KNOCK THE SPOTS OFF" somebody came into usage.

So watch your step…you might stumble into the wrong SPOT, get your SPOTS KNOCKED OFF, be PUT ON THE SPOT, and remember—"X" will mark your final, and perhaps eternal, RESTING SPOT.

Cats And Dogs

"Cats and dogs," they call these places, over on Real Estate Row where the brokers and realtors all gather and the traders and dealers all play.

Over there, CATS AND DOGS are the small parts of the stock-in-trade, the odd lots, the run-of-the-mill, bits and pieces of real property. Individually they don't amount to much because they don't count for much. They've lost out in the push and shove of economic life.

What is it that makes real estate fall out of favor, turn into CATS AND DOGS? Fashion, if it ever flourished here, is gone. Traffic no longer flows past, or perhaps it's been speeded up…dangerously. Maybe the street is roughshod, unfixed, or the buildings front awkwardly on the street—entrances shadowy, queasy-looking, raising questions, doubts.

Five empty storefronts, all in a row. Where did all the customers go? Part of the answer lies in boom and bust. Many CATS AND DOGS are leftovers from a couple of economic booms back, when builders overbuilt one type of structure, and now it's a drug on the market.

Don't look the other way, although most of us do. Fasten your gaze on CATS AND DOGS, tune in on their signals, sometimes subtle, often blatant.

There is dereliction and decrepitude all around. Trash blows down the sidewalk, weeds sprout from the cracks.

See the secondhand furniture shop off the beaten path. The beaten path has fallen off the map, the flow of traffic diverted someplace else.

These CATS AND DOGS don't just happen. They're the right-before-your-eyes products of a market system dominated by fast turnover, a system that feeds on new development, doesn't know when to stop, starves the CATS AND DOGS, and lets its neighborhood go…to the CATS AND DOGS. It's a brutal and, on the whole, predictable system for manufacturing CATS AND DOGS.

Home 2 Place

The Burbs

There's no valid name for it, this huge, generic, man-made place we've got on our hands, in our hands, hovering over our budgets. It's located a short non-rush-hour's drive from a hundred million people—a short run from where they live, work, and have their unquiet being.

The short name for all this is "THE BURBS." But let's try on for size two other, longer names: CITIFIED COUNTRYSIDE, and COUNTRYFIED CITY. In its shortened form, THE BURBS are something short of THE BOONDOCKS and surely not COUNTRY TOWNS. They're an uneasy mix of city and country.

I've just come from a thousand-mile trip across Middle America, following the old national road, U.S. 40, across Illinois, Indiana, Ohio, and into West Virginia. Plenty of COUNTRYSIDE, indeed.

But strung out between towns and cities, slathered across farmstead and crop field, running off to the horizons, are THE BURBS—extenuated, attenuated, proliferating.

Not fully urbanized. And no longer fully agricultural. The number of fulltime working farms in the United States is down around one million today. You can watch them disappearing along U.S. 40. This was once the great axis of production—farm products traveled the road on their way to market. Today it's becoming an axis of consumption, lined with so-called "baby farms," little "homesteads" inhabited by commuters. Is this not the way the whole country is going? From production to consumption? Look at U.S. 40 and decide for yourself.

Center City

Center City, they call it. Center City, the central downtown neighborhood of big-city Philadelphia. But if you associate big city with riot and ruckus, think again.

I recently returned from a week in Center City Philadelphia, and frankly, I didn't know there was such a fascinating place left so clearly flourishing and intact in the United States.

Seventy thousand people live in Center City Philadelphia. Let me tell you what it's like, briefly. My wife and I stayed with friends, a working couple. On a cobblestone, one-lane street with a sidewalk barely two feet across. In a house that's only twelve feet wide, the so-called "holy trinity"—three rooms, one on top of the other. Built in 1830, that is, EIGHTEEN thirty! Our hosts managed to buy the house next door so they now have twenty-four feet of frontage—think of it—on a one-lane street. The "backyard" is a tiny patio overlooked by neighbors.

With neighbors close by, they visit back and forth. They close off the little street around the corner for kids' playtime. Around another corner is the subway, then a grocery, dry cleaners, hardware store, rental agency, repair shop, and a coffee bar. On the corner you can buy the Philadelphia, New York, Wall Street newspapers, and the local gay weekly.

To get downtown, we walked just a few blocks to the closest skyscrapers. To dinner we walked a brightly lighted mile, crossing Independence Square and other historic spots along the way.

Everywhere we walked, there were "eyes-on-the-street," people watching people...homeowners, renters, shoppers, downtown workers doing late-afternoon shopping. There were shop owners and tourists like us. So, If you haven't noticed that Center City is alive and well, try Philadelphia.

Disorder

What impressed me when I first met Tom Odum was the way he compressed all of nature's energies into language. A large, red-headed, forceful, opinionated, unforgettable man…member of a distinguished Southern family of scientists.

I like to describe Tom Odum as an inventor tracking and tracing the networks and pathways of energy as it flows through the landscape.

What we call "American" weather, Tom Odum points out, is really un-American—its explosive energies imported from Siberia, Alaska, and the Caribbean, captured in the mix-master of mid-America climate, and caught up in the competition among television weathercasters.

Odum's way of looking at the self-organization of nature—everything getting energies from someplace else—comes to mind when I stand by my little Kentucky limestone spring. For my little fresh-water, running-water spring has its beginnings half a world beyond my property line. It is "made" in the Asiatic-Arctic cold and Caribbean heat. They mix to become rainfall across the Ohio Valley, forty-four inches per year upon the quarter square mile of this 19th-century suburban watershed.

This little stream is a setup for DISORDERLY conduct in my backyard. Kids play in it, dogs splash in it, birds drink and flutter and wash in it. I disturb its peace with my high-tech associate, a Sears-Roebuck electric pump, powered by coal from Appalachia. And with that pump, I manipulate the food chain as I irrigate my garden.

And so, come rain or shine, my garden is bright with foreign imports—the Toyotas and Hondas of my seed catalog—California cantaloupes, squash from Central America, potatoes from the Andes, weeds from Europe, and flowers from the far corners of the earth.

I do what all gardeners do—upset the balance of nature. I trouble the ground with fork and spade. With mechanical helpers, I fight the natives who got here first—I've been trained to call them "weeds," "plants out of place."

Like all gardens, mine is temporary. It depends on large annual injections of human and mechanical energy from elsewhere. I tap into the worldwide storm of garden information that pulses through the media.

Here, in a universe forever seeking to return to what we call "DISORDER," we arrive at our very own handiwork—a lovely little bit of temporary, man-made order. And that is what we call "The Garden."

Downtown

Most stories about DOWNTOWN begin down at the landing, down by the docks, down at the water's edge, or down at the tidewater. That was where most early American settlers arrived by boat. Their descendants still celebrate Pioneers' Day down at the Town Landing, and in New England they still talk about going "down-city."

"Going DOWNTOWN" still means just that—going downhill. My grandfather walked a mile downhill to his office in DOWNTOWN Macon, Georgia, just blocks from the old Indian river crossing and town landing. He only began to feel his age when the afternoon walk uphill to College Street left him "puffing and blowing like a porpoise."

Some folks still think DOWNTOWN is strictly a by-product of unique, local get up and go, independent of outside systems and forces. Partly true. Many a small town of the 19th century could become the echo of one determined man or gang who could whip a settlement into town shape.

Some hotshot corporations still make a big footprint DOWNTOWN: Humana in Louisville; Cummins Engine in Columbus, Indiana; Whittle Communications in Knoxville; Petro-Chemicals in Houston.

But now information and capital flow around the world by satellite and fax machines. DOWNTOWN is no longer the only game in town. And when Detroit, Washington, D.C., and Los Angeles erupted with underclass riots close to the city centers, the old DOWNTOWN battened down as a tight security zone.

The biggest casualty of over-security is street life. Pedestrians get shunted into underground tunnels or second-story skyways. Flagship buildings get designed like citadels, with in-house cafeterias, in-house shops, and only one doorway per block. DOWNTOWN is undergoing depopulation…by design.

The Garden

Spring never promised to come on time, so while the worst of winter surrounds us, now's the time to check out seed catalogs, planting schedules, and to hope against hope that spring and GARDENS are just around the corner.

What's a GARDEN? It's the height of human arrogance—artificial, contrived, an intrusion upon Nature. Our intruder ancestors cleared forests in Europe and irrigated deserts in the Middle East thousands of years ago. Now herbicides and insecticides zap the bugs and weeds, and thousands of books at libraries and Hawley-Cooke tell us how to manage wind and weather, how to persuade flowers and veggies to do our bidding, and how to chop and till and trouble the ground.

Last week at the National Farm Machinery Show at the state fairgrounds, I patted a hay-baling machine two stories high. You'd pay $168,000 to pull this complex machine across your hay field and roll the hay into bales.

But a GARDEN needs something much more complex—a treaty between you and a patch of sunlight and the good earth. So to get ready for spring, prepare to seize the first bright and sunny day. Pick a sturdy, lightweight chair. Take it and try it out-of-doors. Move it around until the light, the air, the space, the view, all together feel just right in that particular place. That's Item Number One in the treaty between you and the territory. Once you find the outdoor spot to relax in, there's bound to be a good spot for a GARDEN plot close by, a place for you to dig, a place for nature to deliver. So, have a good season.

Digging The Cosmos

It's March and we stand in the garden, my shovel and I, waiting for spring. The shovel is in my hands, a bit shabby from season after season digging into history.

Beneath my feet the soil is a fertile, friable, shovel-happy dark, rich garden mixture. Man-made stuff. I've been composting sixteen years, now. If this were seventeenth century France and I were to move to another place, I'd have the legal right to take up my topsoil—MY topsoil—and take it with me.

Composting, as I do it, means collecting and saving stuff we once threw away: vegetable waste from the kitchen, leaves and trash from the yard, rotted sawdust, grass clippings, wood ashes, and any horse and cow manure I can get.

I stand on cosmopolitan soil, shipped in from faraway to decompose and make fertile this place...artichokes from California; oranges from Texas and Florida; bananas from Central America; coffee grounds from Costa Rica and Hawaii; presidential peanut shells, perhaps from Jimmy Carter's peanut farm in Plains, Georgia.

Sparkling up at me are bits of mica dust from the mica mines of North Carolina, 400 miles away, where the roadsides glitter in the sunshine, bright with mica dust.

I dig up another shovelful...soft, crumbly leaf mold, collected in plastic leaf bags from Crescent Hill, St. Matthews, and Cherokee Triangle...stuff people threw away...for my cosmopolitan garden.

I dig another shovelful of Elsewhere—topsoil washed down off a nearby hillside. I dig it from the low spot where it settles, a dozen wheelbarrow loads of topsoil every year—for my cosmopolitan compost.

These are friendly cosmopolitans, come to rest and to make fertile my next garden as we stand here in the cosmos, my shovel and I, waiting for spring.

Right Here

Thanks for joining us HERE to deal with the question WHY.

Why is it most of us, our voices dripping with sympathy, will say "THERE, THERE!" instead of saying "HERE, HERE!"? And why do we say "HERE! HERE!" as a form of command, as when we summon up an uppity puppy?

That question set me to wondering about HERE, which is not the same thing as wandering HERE and there, and before I knew it, I was buried up to HERE in the subject.

For most of us, HERE is located about one inch behind the bridge of the human nose. All directions start RIGHT HERE. All spaces, all places, are judged by where they are in relation to, and when seen from, RIGHT HERE, or as they say in some parts of Appalachia, "ROT CHEER."

Each of us judges the world and its directions from our very own, personal HERE and now. So we say, "Imagine seeing you HERE!" And the other responds, " HERE, of all places!" When we shake hands we say, "Put it HERE!" A newcomer might say, "HERE I come, ready or not." If there's a crowd, we say, "Well, we're all HERE now."

We take a drink and say "HERE's to you," or sometimes "HERE's looking at you." Or, as Humphrey Bogart said, unforgettably, in "Casablanca," "HERE's looking at you, Kid!"

If the other person talks nonsense, we say, "That's neither HERE nor there." And if the other goes too far, gets out-of-line, you might say, "not HERE," or maybe "not done HERE!" If one person goes a bit too far too fast, the other might say "HERE now," which is to say, "Stop that HERE and now!" On the other hand, if you're both going too far, one of you might say "HERE we go again!"

And that's the view from that place called "HERE."

What Goes Here

"Imagine seeing you here!" That's the way many a conversation gets started in places that are special, unexpected, or unusual. But "Imagine seeing you here!" is said sardonically, if not sarcastically, when here is the same old here where you met the last time.

So, you're fed up with banality, with saying, "Well, here we are again!" Or with the triteness of asking, brightly—when you know the answer already—"What brings you here?" Or the futility of saying "Imagine seeing you here," when everybody around you and everybody you know has been here in this place all their born days. But what else do you say for openers?

If you're both fast-track operators, you can say, "here today, gone tomorrow." If the other person just might remember the famous quote by American General Pershing in the first World War, while landing with fresh American troops in France, you could try "LaFayette, we are here!"

There might be an occasion, although it doesn't come readily to mind, for picking up on a once-popular radio show and saying, "Duffee ain't here." Or, straggling back a few more years, "here comes de Judge!" Or from children's games called "Here Comes a Duke," or "Here Come Fifty Men to Work," or "Here Comes a Bluebird."

Suppose the conversation takes a political turn. You can borrow from President Harry Truman's "The buck stops here." Or from the novelist James Jones, "From Here to Eternity." Or celebrate the late arrival of a friend with the salutation "Heeeeeeeerrrre's Johnny."

Or, to jump the season a bit, "here we go, gathering nuts in May."

ICEHOUSES

There's a unique place, the only one I know about, out on the edge of town, that bears witness to days gone by, when people made natural ice out in the open air, long before mechanical refrigeration.

That reminder of those past days stands on the grounds of an historic country house called "Farmington," a Southern brick mansion of the Speed family, built in 1810.

A few hundred feet from the big house stands the rebuilt ruin of an ICEHOUSE. And there they stored wintertime ice cut from a freshwater pond close by.

Judging from its size, it held enough ice to last a big household through a long hot summer. It's bigger than most ICEHOUSES that show up in an 1881 book called *Barns, Sheds, and Outbuildings of the United States*.[1]

Lest we forget, that was the only way to enjoy ice in the summertime heat, up till a century ago. If you built a modest 20 x 16 x 10-foot-high ICEHOUSE, you could store sixty tons of ice. For insulation, you'd need twenty-five wagonloads of sawdust.

That was back when, a century ago, natural ice was a major crop exported from the United States, packed in sawdust and stored over winter in an ICEHOUSE, then shipped, mostly out of Boston, to places like Havana, Cuba, where it brought a hefty price. Fresh Pond, now part of Boston's suburban water system, once had its own ice-manufacturing depot, its ice packed up and shipped out by trainloads and then by ship.

Today, ice ponds are strictly for skaters. In winters like 1978, every pond or lake or stretch of open creek turns into a highway for ice skating, and even this far south, for ice boating.

If you had used this year's big freeze—down to twenty-two degrees below zero—to store your own ice, you'd have more than enough for next summer's "bourbon and branch water." But... where would you have found twenty-five wagonloads of sawdust?

1: Republished 1977 by Stephen Greene Press, Brattleboro, VT 05301.

Mom And Pop Peckerwood
Roadside Multiple Enterprise Zone

You don't find it along every roadside. But when you do, put on the brakes, pull off the road, come to a full stop. Get out. That's the only way to appreciate the full extent and deep-rooted indigenosity of the Mom and Pop Peckerwood Roadside Multiple Enterprise Zone. It stretches down the roadside the length of three football fields...a combination flea market, curbside showcase, and repair shop for whatever drives in.

It's a regional specialty along southern state highways, but is also penetrating New England. Its roots go back to the Great Depression and wagon trains to the West.

This one started when Mom and Pop, fresh out of World War II, bought five acres of scrub land from their cousin real cheap—the cousin and the land—and set up a weekend flea market.

Done real good, as they like to say. Soon enough, open for business seven days a week. Son Number One, fresh out of the Army, set up a fish-bait, soft-drink stand and before you could say "franchise," he was dealing chainsaws and posthole diggers. Son Number Two, back from Vietnam, dug up two old gasoline pumps, dug them in, hired a mechanic, and had himself a semi-hemi-quasi full-service Truck Stop.

Today Mom and Pop offer black-velvet paintings, white-fuzzy-wooly teddy bears, hot meals, shotguns, and soda pop. Grandson runs the store, a second cousin's cashier, and Pop...he's off at the county seat—at his age!—bangin' on the table to get rezoning.

That's the way it goes, for now, out at the Mom And Pop Peckerwood Roadside Multiple Enterprise Zone.

MEGACITY

If you looked at it for the very first time—that word spelled M-E-G-A-C-I-T-Y—and if you found it to be a total stranger, might you not be forgiven for pronouncing it me-GASS-ity? If you did that, you would put it, and yourself, in good linguistic company—along with words like caPASSity, raPASSity, auDASSity, menDASSity, not to mention that place called the SarGASSo Sea—all of these being words where the accent goes up in the middle.

So how come, all of a sudden, when we get to M-E-G-A-C-I-T-Y, we downshift it from meGASSity, haul the accent back up front, and call it "MEGA-city"? Let's leave that messy mega-question to dangle a bit while we deal a bit, plus a dash of double-dealing, with the question: is Louisville a MEGACITY? Has it grown beyond all recognition into a regional constellation? Does it have anything in common with that string of cities from Boston to Washington now called "MEGACITY," or the slightly longer MEGALOPOLIS?

One attraction of the name MEGALOPOLIS is that it raises none of the pronunciational questions I just raised about MEGACITY—that is, the possibility of mispronouncing it "meGASSity."

Once you look at MEGALOPOLIS and once you admit it's a real word (its antecedents in Greek go back three thousand years), then you need not stumble along it, but gallop along it, take it in stride.

So…is Louisville part of a MEGALOPOLIS? The answer is decidedly NOT! The closest real MEGALOPOLIS is 700 miles thataway, eastward around Washington, D.C. and extending north to Boston.

The closest thing we've got to a pale version of MEGALOPOLIS in this part of the United States is the tail end of the Cleveland-Columbus-Dayton-Cincinnati urbanized corridor. And when I say it ends at Cincinnati, I refer to the Kentucky counties south of Cincinnati's suburbs, where you literally fall off the edge of the urbanized universe into flat-out, way-out, straight-out, thinned-out, up-and-down Real Country—backwoods and boondocks; the open, woodsy outback of Middle America in the Upper-South.

Whatever passes for a Midwestern MEGALOPOLIS comes full stop in Northern Kentucky.

And a hundred miles further, down here, out here, Louisville stands anything BUT self-sufficient, alone amidst and amongst its competing suburbs. And beyond them the thinly populated countryside. None of these places are part of any great MEGALOPOLIS.

In all directions there is Real Country and then, off a hundred miles or more thisaway-thataway, Nashville, Indianapolis, Cincinnati.

So here we stand in the Louisville area. If not MEGACITY then what? Here we have a collection of communities trying to get together by passing the plate, without a common church. A bi-state, five-county constellation, all interconnected, tied together; yet foolishly, jealously, each trying to go it alone, pulling and hauling in a hundred self-centered, self-serving directions. NOT part of MEGALOPOLIS. Let's get that out of the way. But we ARE, unavoidably, a metropolitan area. How we make it work is the real question for the future.

Our Town

There's no way to talk in public about OUR TOWN but up-beat, up-market, in the upper register. Sociologically speaking, we like to say OUR TOWN is upwardly mobile, and if things aren't going just right, well, we'll come up with something.

OUR TOWN, when it gets written up by OUR TOWN's newspaper, is fundamentally OK. If somebody in the big world out there writes bad things about OUR TOWN, well, they're just down on us, down at the mouth, down at the heels, going through their old put-down routine.

Because OUR TOWN, well, sure it's got a few things wrong with it, yeah. But we'll fix 'em up soon enough, won't we? We'll show 'em, those Fancy Dans and troublemakers out to get us down.

Because OUR TOWN is really a nice place once you get to know it, know the ropes, don't get out of line. Just don't pay any attention to what they say in the big city newspapers and on TV. They're just a bunch of sensationalists, we all know that, don't we?

We know where it is, but you may not find it on the map—that invisible line around OUR TOWN. We on this side—inside. All in here together. And THEY—all THEM, THE OTHERS, THE REST, OUTSIDERS—are on the Other Side, the Outside.

That's the basic geography lesson they teach, almost without words, in OUR TOWN. And when they stop talking that kind of basic geography, it's no longer OUR TOWN...right?

Sand Castles

It's still being debated among the growing breed of SAND CASTLERS in America whether Leonardo da Vinci cast models in sand of his famous works in Italy. What is not debatable is the growing fad, call it a competitive sport, of building castles in the sand—no dream, but a full-time, competitive business.

These are no longer little diddly, piddly piles in the wet, but are works of ephemeral landscape art. You're seeing landscape in the making. Some SAND CASTLES extend for miles along a beach, disappearing overnight when the tide comes in. This fits artist George Roualt's observation: "Art is never finished, only abandoned."

SAND CASTLING moved out of family vacations to become a verb and a fad. It went big time in—you guessed it—Fort Lauderdale, Florida, back in 1952. It drew spectators by the thousands, and acquired international media personalities, cult figures like Todd Vander Pluys, who got a fee of $120,000 for a 120-foot row of buildings at, of all places, the dry-as-dust city of Albuquerque, New Mexico. A SAND CASTLE in Japan set a record at fifty-six feet and two inches high. Among the more popular formations are fortifications, cathedrals, pyramids, the Seven Dwarfs, dragons, snakes, and reclining mermaids. Please do not handle!

Its experts barnstorm the country. Some build their castles, not in barns, not in Spain, but in shopping centers in the interest of crowd building and cash flow. It's come a long way from the beach.

SKYLINE

Somewhere near the top of every civic booster's shopping list, somewhere up there amongst the stratospheric pitches of bond-issue salesmen, there occurs that electrifying word "SKYLINE." A city without a SKYLINE, they say, is no city at all. The center can't hold without a SKYLINE. A downtown without a SKYLINE is a contradiction in terms.

SKYLINES tell stories of downtowners' derring-do with an unlimited line of credit. A symbol of Progress with a capital "P." Playground for the godly architect and the ambitious corporation. SKYLINE's got to provide plenty of executive suites with panoramic views from the fortieth floor—and up.

Photographed from a distance, a SKYLINE is designed to impress. If your building's not on the SKYLINE yet, you assemble electronic imagery and fake it in a four-color magazine ad.

By 1992 many SKYLINES were hard to tell apart. Robin Garr says Louisville, Kentucky, shares "generic SKYLINE" with Buffalo and Sacramento. One could add many others.

In New York's Manhattan, the SKYLINE has magnetized footloose capitalists from all over the world. Each signature tower tries to up-sky and outdo the last. And so, Manhattan sidewalks and streets are shadowed, as though you'd picked up Manhattan by the scruff of the neck, or SKYLINE, and moved it northward, away from the sun.

Philadelphia once had a rule: no skyscrapers higher than the statue of William Penn on top of City Hall. That rule went bust in the 1980s. It's clear that city plans, earthquakes, plane crashes, and King Kong have NOT cured the itch to wipe out more sky with an ever-expanding SKYLINE.

Soho

"Oh, please tell me," breathed the bright-eyed young hat-checker in a downtown restaurant after she had encountered my uncontrollable itch to talk about cities. "What's going to happen to Bardstown Road?"

Now, Bardstown Road is a universal type: once upon a time just a busy old 19th-century country road radiating out of my city, pointed toward and named for a once-distant county-seat town. As late as the 1880s Bardstown Road was dusty with cattle being driven to market in Butchertown.

Now it's a busy-bee-hivey strip, midday traffic doing lunch, bookstores, restaurants, discos, night spots. Bright lights on the sidewalks, wine and cheese when the galleries do a launch.

"But is it going to STAY safe?" said my bright young interlocutor. Looking into those lovely eyes, I forgot to mention that famous London neighborhood called "SoHO". Great mansions built on Soho Square in London in the 1700s. It went downhill until, in the time of Charles Dickens, it was a refuge for homeless men. But by the late 1800s it had become the haunt of famous writers, not too far from the great shopping arcades of Regent Street, with apartments overlooking the scene.

So what does this say for strips like Bardstown Road or the newly gentrifying Frankfort Avenue in Louisville?

Exactly what I (think I) said to the bright-eyed young woman handing me my coat: "So long as Bardstown Road and Frankfort Avenue keep plenty of folks living alongside, next door, within walking distance, their eyes on the street; so long as it does NOT turn into an exclusively business street chopped up by parking lots, with nobody home, nobody close by, nobody jogging, walking their dogs, stopping to chat, nobody to cover the sidewalks with sociability; so long as stable neighborhood life and its cloak of protection reach out over the street, it IS a safe place to be, to see, and to be seen."

SPRINGHOUSE

Nestled and tucked away, way back in the outback, in the farthest corner of the place where I live, there lies a little SPRINGHOUSE made of blocks of local limestone. And if the term "SPRINGHOUSE" is seldom sprung on you, if it sounds old-fashioned, harking back to the 19th century, let me fill you in. For SPRINGHOUSES have been around ever since the first primitive man piled one stone on top of another to make a wall—one of prehistory's great moments of invention thousands of years ago.

But this stone SPRINGHOUSE, my very own, is only one generation old, barely into adolescence; the first stone SPRINGHOUSE built in my neighborhood in perhaps a hundred years.

The stone came from three wrecking jobs around town: stone foundations from Smoketown and Butchertown and from an old barn in St. Matthews. Today it houses—that is to say, it shelters from strangers and outsiders—a real, live, flowing, running water spring that pours, all sprightly with exuberance, out from the basic limestone that supports the landscape that is my neighborhood.

Below the SPRINGHOUSE is a tiny pond and a trickling stream that nourish watercress in season, that support hundreds of birds flying in and out all day. The pond was discovered this summer by mallard ducks who took a splash and decided it was too small. But they keep flying in. Do they hope it'll expand, just for their sake?

Perhaps you have a spring or know of a spring. That's precious knowledge, for there's no official record showing how many springs still spring in our county.

So, if you do have one, if you know of one, do what you can to keep it from the fate of most springs—trashed by neighbors, bulldozed back underground by land developers. You, too, can be a spring saver in your own neighborhood. Give it a try.

Where Louisville Begins

I've been looking for the places where my hometown, Louisville, begins…those points where it registers on newcomers, those spots which, by means of signs, symbols, shouts, commotion, or by the silent prompting of geographic fact say, "You have arrived, you are here, this is Louisville!"

And are these hard to find! The other day I made a thirty-mile sweep up and down the northern approaches to Louisville—chiefly the big artery of Interstate 65, which funnels major north-south traffic across the great Ohio River into Louisville.

Had I been a stranger and not an inveterate map reader, I'd have been hard put to know not only where I was, but where Louisville was.

Where is Colonel Harlan Sanders in his big white suit, here where we need him? The roadside offers no big hello, no visible glad hand, no visual jumping up and down to let interstate travelers know that just ahead lies the Gateway to the South, the largest city on this highway once you've made it past Indianapolis—the Bourbon Capital, amateur Volleyball Capital, Horse Racing Capital, and other capitals holding uncashed tickets to the front row.

Travelers can discover for themselves a city that has mastered the art of self-concealment. This has one of the most dramatic skylines on the American heartland river system, but no sign on that skyline to identify just exactly what place this is.

One lonesome, itsy-bitsy sign that says, "Welcome to Kentucky" is stuck up among the girders on the interstate bridge, right above the busiest, most stressful traffic lane of the bridge. Slow down and miss your turn. Read it at your risk.

So where is Louisville? Tucked away in our little corner of the universe, the very picture of self-concealing anonymity.

THE PLACE

"This is THE PLACE," said a small group of us in Louisville, with some braggadocio, as we tried to persuade the U.S. Atomic Energy Commission to locate a diffusion plant, a so-called "billion-dollar facility," here in 1965. "THIS IS THE PLACE" was the name of a boastful booklet published by *The Courier-Journal*.

"This is THE place," said Brigham Young, founding father of the Mormon Church, father of I-don't-know-how-many children by how-many wives, and founder of Salt Lake City.

What's so special about the "THE"—spelled with a capital T and an H and an E? When you stick that word "THE" in front of person, place, or thing, you attach to it a singularity and special prestige.

"THE" makes it hot. Adding "THE" is one of those little routines we go through to single out a place, such as THE Bluegrass, to enhance it; to expand its influence; broaden its reach beyond a single, individual case. "Bluegrass," unmodified, is music or vegetation. THE Bluegrass is THE PLACE.

It's got status that we attach to it when we "put the THE to it." That's what THE Beatles, THE Grateful Dead, THE Beach Boys, and THE Who were up to.

"THE" is what linguists call a "function word." Most of us use it as a conversational signal that the noun coming next refers to one of a kind, something unique, special, like THE Riviera or its down-home cousin, THE Redneck Riviera, or THE universe or THE ocean. Here little ole three-letter THE takes on a big job—"to indicate generic rather than individual application."

Going generic is a way of going big time, upscale, uptown. It adds emphasis, intense designation. Adding the THE helps do it. So watch out you don't misuse it to muddy THE waters.

Town Creek

Town creek. It's gone thataway. Straight down. Underground. Lost but not forgotten. Diverted, but still there, seeping and flowing its way underground, downstream. Only gravity knows it's down there, unsung and unknown by present generations.

Town creek. It's the reason the town got to be where it's at in the first place. Back then, it was the town's only water supply. Like as not, the town spring ran into town creek, and that's why the first settlers stopped—cool, clear waters, shaded by a giant tree.

That's where town creek began. That's where the town began. Dig deep through the old records or dig under that new parking lot behind the courthouse and you'll find it. One early town creek, called "Minetta Creek," in New York's Manhattan, still runs, far below, as it twists around subways and foundations.

A little way out of town the first Lovers Lane went down by the town creek, back when the woods were green, when shadows fell, and two hearts beat as one.

I once tried to follow historic Hangman's Creek in the old gold-mining town of Placerville, California. Gone, most of it, under streets, a railroad, a motel.

But some town creeks do hang on. In Boulder, Colorado, I wandered along Boulder Creek, the center and pride of the city. I even joined a local crew to go white-water rafting through a protected, open greenway. The rule here is: if you know one, save one. Nobody's making any more of those wonderful places called "town creeks."

Uptown

We now embark on a merry chase called "going UPTOWN." But before we go, somebody's bound to ask, as I myself asked, what's so UP about UPTOWN? What's the difference between UPTOWN and DOWNTOWN across the country?

Those who follow the whims and pleasures of these crossings recall that most DOWNTOWNS were down by the river, down by the docks, down by the original town landing, down where it all began. That was, and is, the location of downtown in most older seaboard and river cities.

But some cities didn't start that way at all. They got their start where two Indian paths came together—on high ground. Indians were no fools. They picked dry land, which was usually high land.

Charlotte, North Carolina, is just such a city, founded where two Indian trails crossed—on high ground. Its downtown has been called "UPTOWN" since day one.

And Charlotte is the only major city I know of in America where the local newspaper has an official lexicographic policy of always referring to UPTOWN in its news columns. It changed its stylebook and went public in 1987. This usage "…is reinforced by the fact that people going to Charlotte's central business district from any point in town had to go uphill," said associate editor Jack Claiborne.

Other towns and cities may, and do, get into the one-upmanship game, place naming fancy suburbs or high-ground locations or upscale shopping districts UPTOWN. But the ones with the best claim to UPTOWN are those, like Charlotte, that actually began at an UP location, thanks to Indians who wanted to keep their feet dry.

Walking Distance

How many of us—how many of you—are within WALKING DISTANCE of a neat place to go walking with a friend to dinner or to a quick-in take-out snack bar? Or a neighborhood place to get a loaf of bread and spool of thread—using that threadbare expression as our shopping list? Or a haircut, hairdo, tank of gas, or a gallon of milk? Or to get something fixed, or to buy a stamp?

For millions of folks, WALKING DISTANCE is a measure of the good life. It's cheap, quick, non-polluting. WALKING DISTANCE covers about four square miles of territory, say within a one-mile radius of where one lives. That's a fifteen-minute walk for most adults.

If you're unlucky and have no choice in the matter, WALKING DISTANCE can be risky, full of hazards, where the street is a threat. Or if you have opted for suburbia, there's no choice but to get in your car and drive off and away—driving distance.

But let me get down to particulars—where WALKING DISTANCE still works. Within fifteen minutes' WALKING DISTANCE of where I have chosen to live and write, there's a railroad track, hardware store, large drugstore, five eating places, two bookshops, three churches, fire station, community center, two public schools, wine shop, postal facility, and several fax machines. And perhaps a thousand households—including those of several good friends.

Did you notice? I've said nothing about work places, for I am one of the growing millions who work at home. How few of us any longer have a job within WALKING DISTANCE of where we live? WALKING DISTANCE is a place where work place need not be kept distanced from home place by the long commute, the pileup on the bridge, the rush-hour combat zone they call "the interstate."

WALKING DISTANCE can be a universal measure of the good life. Isn't it time that the next time you consider making a move you try on WALKING DISTANCE for comfort and for size? It's a good way to measure the world to suit yourself.

Venues

Bonfire

Comes now the season, and come all ye to light up and gather 'round the BONFIRE. It's romantic, it's picturesque, but, what with fire regulations, most city folk have to retreat indoors if they've got a fireplace, if they've got firewood. That's a long way from the hoarse, deep roar and the rumble, the crackle and the grumble, and the primitive power of a real BONFIRE.

It was not always thus so timid, thus so tame. Back in pagan times, back in the Middle Ages, folks held BONFIRES to celebrate the end of the longest day of the year, December 21. Or the arrival of spring or heathenish events long lost in the mists of time. There were sparkling embers shooting sky-high, towering pillars of flame, shouts and routs and roustabouts, and an oversupply of drinking and rassling that coulda turned into fist fighting or lovemaking or just…ah…fooling around.

Back as early as 1473 it was spelled B-A-N-E-F-I-R-E in Scotland, and down to about 1760 it was spelled B-O-N-E-F-I-R-E. People saved up and gathered up old cattle bones to burn in BONEFIRES…a European custom till around 1800.

Today, what's left? Outdoor BONFIRES against the law in most populated counties. Cattle skeletons you can still find in the backwoods a half hour from where I speak. But no BONFIRE to burn up the bones.

In a few places, such as along the Mississippi River in St. James Parish, Louisiana, BONFIRES do carry on as a community get-together.

On Christmas Eve, humongous BONFIRES by the dozens. Folks hauling burnables by the truckload. You can see them miles away, those brightly burning, remote tail endings of a custom ancient as mankind.

CAPITALS

Now for a short cruise among the new CAPITALS, spelled with an A-L-S. I'm told by well-placed informants that the CANOE CAPITAL of America is Milton, Florida, on the Black River; that the CHOLESTEROL CAPITAL, stretching the term somewhat, is the entire state of Wisconsin; that Bridgeport, Connecticut, was recently labeled as the BANKRUPTCY CAPITAL; and Fontana, California, is CAPITAL OF THE FOG BELT.

From Alabama we've got these capital grabbers: Henegar is POTATO CAPITAL of the South; and Albertville, FIRE HYDRANT CAPITAL of the world.

Now for the BANK ROBBERY CAPITAL of America. It was christened on May 29, 1992, when "five groups of bank robbers...invaded five Los Angeles banks." According to Jim Newton of the *Los Angeles Times*, "It was, as far as officials can tell, the worst day for 'takeover' bank robberies...in Los Angeles, which holds the title as America's BANK ROBBERY CAPITAL."

New Jersey's got another candidate...Newark, the AUTO THEFT CAPITAL of the country.

And consider Austin, Texas, the BAT CAPITAL of the United States. Every evening, one-and-a-half million bats fly in and out of crevices in the Congress Avenue Bridge over the Colorado River. Folks by the hundreds gather, some to collect bat guano, some to watch bats. Restaurants do business CAPITALizing on bat watchers. For this kind of CAPITAL formation you need a good batting average.

Casino Landing

There's gonna be a new place in town. It's still in the making, just in the offing, called "CASINO LANDING." I suggest we get used to the sound of it, because from the looks of it, CASINO LANDING is becoming part of the local geography.

CASINO LANDING isn't yet on the map, and its actual legal status is debatable. But there's no question that people around here with a well-located waterfront are looking at converting it to one or more CASINO LANDINGS.

If you thought gambling is something you do only on track or off track, there's a new game a-comin' to town. It's the latest version of a riverboat gambling casino—tied up, anchored, hitched, or otherwise connected to a CASINO LANDING place on the Ohio River.

Once upon a time there were gambling casino ships operating out of Los Angeles harbor at San Pedro, California. Gambling, as well as drinking during Prohibition, was illegal in California. So the ships took on passengers and cruised out beyond the Three Mile Limit into what were called "international waters," where American law didn't apply. The gambling ships advertised daily cruises "to nowhere," where you could drink and gamble all you wanted.

But along this internal waterway there's no nowhere except for that narrow little strip of riverbank in Indiana that's beyond the river territory of Kentucky.

So when gambling casinos nuzzle up to the first CASINO LANDING on the Indiana shore and take their cut and bag their loot, that will be yet another variation of a trip to nowhere.

CURBSIDE

CURBSIDE: One word. Officials in your city and mine have long been telling us what to do at CURBSIDE. From "Curb your Dog" to "No Parking on Sidewalk," down to the latest advisory to people who pick through trash at CURBSIDE: "Steal a Can, Go to Jail."

That's a clue to the small revolution in property rights going on at CURBSIDE.

Now, to zoom in on that particular generic place: CURBSIDE is the narrow strip of public land, often with grass that needs cutting, between the street curbing and the sidewalk. The term also covers the sidewalk just next to the curbing. That's where city hall tells us, or the janitor, or the kids, to put out garbage cans and trash bags, to be picked up by garbage haulers.

As the recycling of glass, of tin and aluminum cans, of cardboard, plastic, and old newspapers slowly gets to be a profitable business, CURBSIDE becomes a zone of competition. Your city or mine may collect that stuff, sort it out, sell it off.

But there's no profit in it unless the city gets ALL recyclables to sort and resell. So the city lawyers declare; CURBSIDE is city turf. The moment you stash a recyclable at CURBSIDE, it's no longer yours. Your kids can't have it. You can't take it back. "Steal a Can"—it's now the city's can—"Go to jail."

Now, nobody designed CURBSIDE to become a battleground between us and the city. CURBSIDE turns out to be the latest venue for learning to sort out things we once threw away. Let's simplify matters and call it "CURBSIDE: Classroom for the Future."

THE DARK

Once upon a time, THE DARK was an important part of everyday and every-night life. It was the Devil's domain where witches bubbled their brew, where evil spirits, escapees, refugees, and illicit others all hung out. Where could you skulk, lurk, or hide if not in THE DARK? When, in that unlit long ago, you advised a friend "Be sure to get here before dark," you were talking not schedule, not cocktails, but survival.

But now we've surrendered THE DARK and all its functions, not all of them illegal or dangerous, to the flashlight, the portable lights, to the electric lighting and utility industries.

Millions of towns, cities, suburbs, exurbs, and remote farmsteads are automatically lit at dusk. In much of the eastern United States, there's not much DARK left, and traces are rare in California. THE DARK has been, in effect, bought out, and THE LIGHT moved outdoors at great expense.

On a national scale, THE DARK is becoming an endangered species. Cities such as San Diego, with world-famous observatories nearby at Mount Palomar and Laguna, have declared The Light to be a pollutant of the heavenly skies, and have tried, by law, to preserve THE DARK—their DARK—from local extinction.

So dependent upon artificial light have we become that the prospect of untimely dusk, or—God Forbid—total darkness, has become a threat to every aspect of life. Is it not time to declare light holidays, to reeducate ourselves to navigate and to survive in total darkness so as to preserve our ancient kinship with THE DARK? Or am I just whistling in—what else—THE DARK?

STARLIGHT

There I was, lying flat on my back, just above water level, supine on a boat dock at the edge of Lake Michigan, looking straight up. Looking hard, watching for the great 1993 Meteor Show. It was the night of the shooting stars, the annual Perseid meteor shower.

But while my friends and I lay flat, swapping stale jokes and straining our eyes in THE DARK, something kept intruding into our view. It was THE LIGHT.

There was—in fact, there is—in fact, no true DARK left. It has been taken over by the utility industries. Our sky that night contained a few fleeting clouds that reflected the lights from the bustling resort towns of Petosky and Bayview across Little Traverse Bay.

But Petosky and Bayview refused to stay across the bay. Their streetlights, floodlights, and dock lights intruded into our peripheral vision. The sky, as we watched for meteor tracks, was a shallow bowl gleaming at the edges—Petosky bright and Bayview all aglitter. Our particular, personal DARK was also intruded upon by automobile lights coming up the beach road behind us.

In spite of the light, that was our lucky night. The sky was clear. The meteors DID streak across our little piece of the universe, from top to bottom, three or more streaking at once. Quick as a flash, and then they were gone. There may have been 400 or so, in the Great Out There beyond our limited vision. But even that small display was the most gonzo extravaganza of a sky show I'd encountered since another summer night, years before, when I lay flat on a sandy beach on the coast of Alaska, watching the great, streaking display of the Northern Lights, and, as I said to the lady on my left....

But that's another story.

Downwind

Come, let us now consider that notorious and sometimes noxious if not nauseous place, that avoidance zone, that locale for evasive action called "DOWNWIND"—D-O-W-N-W-I-N-D—that place that's smack in the path of prevailing or temporary winds and whatever they transport from one place to the next.

Now, hostesses and hunters alike all do their work in that risky zone called "DOWNWIND." When she puts together her guest list, a hostess sniffs the political winds. If Mr. So-and-so is in "bad odor," as one says, scratch him off the list. Hunters, when they stalk their quarry, test which way the wind is blowing so as NOT to reveal their presence.

Commanders in the Gulf War and other wars planned their battles so the smoke, and thus some of the confusion of battle, blew TOWARD the enemy. But the plot, as well as the atmosphere, thickens when the source of today's nasty smell, that grimy, gritty cloud of effluvium, comes from your friendly neighborhood chemical complex that keeps thousands of local workers on the payroll and pays lots of taxes. You recall the traditional answer to complaints? "It smells like money."

But by 1988, one-quarter of all Americans were said to be breathing bad air for part of the year. Where there's smoke, there's fire. Something new is in the wind: citizens organizing, calling themselves DOWNWINDERS, determined no longer to be DOWNWINDED.

For the first time in U.S. history, that once ephemeral place called "DOWNWIND" is getting measured, mapped, and politicized. It sends a new message: ask not which way the wind bloweth, but who did it. That's the question that's blowing in the winds of winter and floating with the zephyrs of spring.

FOOTBALL FIELD

How far is "two hoots and a holler"? Just how far is it from here to yonder? Is there, in fact, a universal yardstick for the size of everyday places?

I got my answer in Brazil from an expert at a monster paper mill: "This place," he said, "is as big as three FOOTBALL FIELDS." Aha! That sounded like a universal unit of psycho-geographic size.

A FOOTBALL FIELD, you recall, is 120 yards long including end zones, and 53 yards wide. And look at how widely it gets into print: A radio telescope in West Virginia is said to be half the length of a FOOTBALL FIELD in diameter. The ice on Mount Rainier is about one FOOTBALL FIELD thick. The typical American shopping mall is as big as two FOOTBALL FIELDS—about as far as most shoppers will walk to or from their cars. The minimum safe distance to stay away from an exploding munitions truck is twelve FOOTBALL FIELDS. United Parcel Service has a new sorting house the size of twenty you-know-whats. And columnist Erma Bombeck tells us that as of 1986, "Americans devoured seventy-one FOOTBALL FIELDS of pizza a day."

But a Canadian dean of women pointed out to me this is a macho metaphor, not much used by women. And while it doesn't mean much overseas, FOOTBALL FIELD, we're told, has become one of the most trivial metaphors in our culture.

But consider the jobs it performs...substitute battleground; partial strip tease at halftime; ego testing ground; venue for gamblers; fashion showplace; cash cow for TV; and for most Americans, the biggest crowd scene they'll ever experience.

How many FOOTBALL FIELDS are there in your life?

Golf Course

WARNING: THE FOLLOWING DEFINITION MAY BE DANGEROUS TO YOUR BLOOD PRESSURE, ESPECIALLY IF YOU ARE A GOLFER.

GOLF COURSE: a ballistic missile site, disguised as a pleasure ground. GOLF COURSE DESIGNER: a specialist in optical illusions, in the deceptive handling of distances, in the sly and devious concealment of obstacles. GOLF COURSE ARCHITECT: one who can make lakes disappear or seem to be twice their actual size. It requires skill and experience. A trip to the holiest of holies, St. Andrews in Scotland, helps—as does a bit of magic.

No GOLF COURSE is what it appears to be. That thing called "par" can be a joke, a challenge, or a trophy. Evil spirits arrive to inhabit GOLF COURSE. Its designers purport to interpret whatever genie, spirit, or muse may occupy the place.

As for players: some play the ball, some play the landscape, some play the score. Oh yes, the ball is a means to an end, happy or otherwise.

Putting green? It's the ultimate artifact, the prototype American lawn. Homeowner looks longingly at Putting Green. Homeowner asks, "Why doesn't MY lawn look like that?" And from that question arises sweat, frustration, maybe an early heart attack. What Homeowner forgets is that the greens committee just spent ten thousand dollars making Putting Green look like that.

As for GOLF COURSE SUBDIVISION, it's a gold-plated necklace draped around GOLF COURSE. It's GOLF COURSE that creates the gold plate—lots with "fairway view" worth fifty to one hundred thousand dollars and up.

In good times and bad, the chance to watch grown men and women hitting little white or pink balls across expensive scenery will continue to entice developers through hook and slice, over the rough, and—just maybe—onto THE GREEN.... FORE!

HANGOUT

What is this place called "HANGOUT"? How does it all start, this business (such goings-on!) called "hanging out" among friends? It all begins when two or more male acquaintances turn into friends. They pal around, hang around, fool around together. And if they do it enough, if they find it suitable enough, it's just the right kind of spot enough, for hanging around in. They keep on doing it in one particular, special place.

Those two words, HANG and OUT, have managed to snuggle themselves together into one word. But back in 1937, in the time of H.L. Mencken's great book *The American Language*, he was hyphenating it—"hang-hyphen-out." Mencken observed that the place where tramps and hoboes gather is a jungle or HANGOUT.

Some HANGOUTS magnetize loners to the dark corners. Some HANGOUTS attract consenting partners. There's a fine line between HANGOUT and hideaway. And once the action steps up, you've segued beyond HANGOUT into rendezvous, trysting place, or Lovers Lane.

Along in here, HANGOUT may go public. Success goes to its head and each HANGOUT gets more complex than the last. Now we're into pickup place, pickup bar, watering hole, stamping (sometimes stomping) ground, gathering place, or meeting place. And then an enterprising somebody slaps a designer's label on HANGOUT and it becomes a fashionable watering hole.

And so, right before your eyes, HANGOUT gets transformed. Here come the hangers-on, the pecking order among the preeners and poseurs, the valet parkers, the haughty majordomo, the hoity-toity headwaiter, the dress code, all that apparatus of hierarchy and hauteur.

But by now, the original hangers-out are long gone. And so the eternal cycle—the ins and outs of hanging out—begins all over again. Until the next time around....

Haunts

Don't look now, but places you never thought twice about are becoming HAUNTS, and by HAUNTS I, and others who keep track of such oddities, mean impromptu, happenstantial, and generally unmapped hangouts for special groups of people.

Some of these places, in all innocence, become targets for outsiders bent on mischief. Take rest stop, that most necessary and innocent of all highway conveniences. Outside Washington, D.C., some folks in Howard County look upon rest stops along Interstate 95 as rendezvous for car jackers. They may be paranoid, of course, but community leaders got "upset about reports that the rest areas were being used by prostitutes, drug dealers, and persons trying to sell stolen goods."[1]

Other HAUNTS become turf for competing groups. Consider the brand-new fishing pier at Huntington Beach, California, with fishermen dangling their lines off the pier. Down below, athletic surfers chasing the waves. But it's become surf-turf—both fishermen and surfers claim that the swirling water around the pilings under the pier is their proper HAUNT. Both claim their "rights."

Another sign of the times is a headline in *The Washington Post*: the "Economy [is] Turning Secondhand Shops into Middle Class Haunts." That is, folks who never bought secondhand before now haunt boutiques with names like Second-Time-Around, Play It Again Sports, Act Two....

Places that, for the first time, are being frequented, patronized, haunted by folks who, like the goods they handle, are down on their luck....

1: Dan Byers, in *The Washington Post* p B 7 September 13, 1992.

HINTERLAND

The other day I took a look into the HINTERLANDS—the outer reaches, the uttermost boondocks, the far-out extent, the Great Out There, the ultimate reach of my hometown's commuting fringes. It's a fourth-generation summer resort in Northern Michigan called "Harbor Springs" and its next-door neighbor with the almost unpronounceable name of We-Que-Ton-Sing.

These two are a small part of Louisville's HINTERLAND. Their populations include a number of Louisville families who flock and flurry northward in the summertime.

So what do Harbor Springs and We-que-ton-sing, Michigan, have in common with Bardstown, Shakertown, Lebanon Junction, Kentucky, and Charlestown or Corydon, Indiana? All are part and parcel of Louisville's HINTERLAND. Should their Louisville connection be cut, they would be diminished. Some would, in fact, wither and shrivel and shrink.

They look to Louisville for customers. Shakertown would be in some distress without the Louisville families that come to visit and support. Oldham and Shelby Counties could no longer flourish without the fertilizing flows from Louisville commuters. Most of these HINTERLANDS depend on Louisville as a market for their lumber, cattle, labor, goods, and services—and their amenities

The early-morning highways into Louisville from all directions are jammed with commuters, that is to say, HINTERLANDERS.

This is no put-down expression: the word "hinter" comes from the German, meaning "near," and it's most often used to describe land that backs up a major port.

And that gets us back to Louisville—a major inland port on the Ohio River for goods assembled from, and shipped to, many a HINTERLAND.

So when you hear the words boondocks, backwoods and HINTERLANDS, just remember that no city—least of all this one—is self-sufficient. And that, without cultivating, patronizing, enticing, soliciting, and keeping close contact with its HINTERLAND, this city of Louisville would dry up and disappear.

The Mailboxes

They're stuck up along thousands of miles of North American roadsides—THE MAILBOXES—vital to every suburban or country dwelling cluster. They connect the outback with the up-front, they link boondocks with county seats, they go between here and there. Not so much as a single mailbox in front of one address or perched on old milk cans and one-hoss plows or teetering on a rotten two-by-four....

For I'm talking about THE MAILBOXES, a collectivity. They gang up at intersections, cluster along roadsides outside the built-up cities. They nestle up, side by side, the daily port of call for millions of folks. They shape up into clumps, rows, double rows, two-level rows.

On many a country road they're the only signal a stranger gets that back up the holler, off down the valley, there's a cluster of families who share, if nothing more, THE MAILBOXES.

It's an inevitable place to meet your neighbors. That's where private life goes public, even if only to receive junk mail. There the long arm of the law reaches out to protect little packets of paper stuffed into metal boxes—Steal a Letter, Go to Jail.

Once upon a time, THE MAILBOXES were part of something called "rural free delivery." But the post office no longer talks "RFD." In some new suburbs, they're housed in make-believe cottages in a drive-through "Local Postal Facility." You need a pull-out lane to stop your car, reach out your car window, dial into your lock box, pick up or drop your mail.

The next step is called a "multi-use-community-facility postage-mailing center"—mechanically clanking out stamps, income tax forms, and public notices. Which requires that THE MAILBOXES move off the road and under the roof. So welcome to what the post office is training us for—one-stop pickup, life in cluster style—what the Material Culture people call "Built America." Don't lose your combination!

THE OLYMPICS SITE

Behind the place-name of the city in which Olympic Games are held, there exists briefly and for television purposes, a non-place called "THE OLYMPIC SITE." It may be one vast stadium with ancillary stadia and event places scattered around the city. Or it may include—as in the winter of 1988 at Calgary, Alberta—a domed stadium for skating and hockey, a ski jump some distance away, and a luge run miles away outside the city—all foregathered and described via TV and news accounts as "THE OLYMPIC SITE." Thus has gradually been manufactured a highly negotiable non-place which occurs only in the media.

Ten anthropologists, during the 1984 Los Angeles Olympics, analyzed the whole array of ceremonial packages, ritualistic sequences, litanies, and pronouncements on the field and on TV. They studied the parades, pilgrimages, and performances; the costumes, outfitters, audiences; prop men moving hurdles, smoothing landing places for pole vaulters, and whitewashing track lanes; the grips stage managing cameras and rearranging backdrops. These, in their professional eyes and lingo, were "ritual performances of the world order."

Dozens of performances had been singled out, rearranged, juxtaposed in new array. The Olympics had been transformed, as though a dozen stages had been merged into one, with a unity created electronically as if by magic, untrue to life, on the TV screen. The screens in millions of homes and bars seemed to be the only place where The Olympics actually occurred for the world to watch.

Television had thus managed to fill the vacuum created by exploding The Olympics into a dozen or more photographically segregated and photogenic segments, all occurring separately. Even the major stadium in Los Angeles was so vast that its various events had to be explained by loudspeaker to the scattered audience. Only a wide-angle camera in helicopter or blimp could squeeze all the action into one man-made scene.

Behind the scene there did, however, exist a multitude of hardstands, swimming pools, running tracks, stadia, judges' stands, and finish lines. If one had said, "I'll meet you at the finish line," both partners were certain to meet. Once upon a time the finish line was simply a cotton string hand held across a track. But no longer. Major races in the 1980s required at the finish line an impressive array of judges, stewards, officials, photographers and their equipment, reflective and timing devices, all requiring several hundred square yards of space. To enter, one needed press passes and perks.

Furthermore, as The Olympics adjusted to mass marketing, THE OLYMPICS SITE was redesigned to get the maximum price for high-ticket seats at the finish line, which turned out to be a relaxed place-name indeed. The area of the finish line has become an electronic zone of analysis and celebration, the focus of actions, actors, laws, regulations, high-tech operators, and deep-pocket contractors.

Thus THE OLYMPICS SITE now viewed worldwide is wholly prefabricated, assembled for telecast, with its components spread over a metropolitan region. It's a long way from that little town in Greece where it all began.

The Great Outdoors

So...it's a beautiful day. You're going into THE GREAT OUTDOORS? But gotta change into something more comfortable? Forgot the suntan lotion, the bug killer, the poncho? Your friend's got an appointment back indoors? So maybe THE GREAT OUTDOORS can wait?

You're in good company—a bona fide member of The Insulated Society, taking part in The Indoorsing of America. It's built up since the 19th century, when sanitation and reform swept the streets clean of beggars, peddlers, garbage, kids, waifs, strays, and tramps. Off into institutions. Prostitutes and other sidewalk salespeople got licensed or expelled.

Air conditioning moved two generations indoors. Your taxes promote the indoorsing of sports into arenas, superdomes, and local versions of Madison Square Garden. Shopping malls and multi-use complexes capture customers, keep them spinning around, spending time and money indoors.

Grief, an ancient form of disturbing the peace, is discouraged in public. Funerals move into funeral parlors, the graveside concealed in a prefab. Drinking is an indoor art form. Outdoor exercise moves into fitness centers. State and County Fairs, remnants of the Middle Ages' carnival spirit, get indoorsed.

For every car, a carport; for every party, a party room; for garden lovers, the garden room. In the TV room, television takes up six hours of couch-potato time per day.

Instead of stepping out, we snuggle down. Thus we insulate ourselves against new experience. We ensure against accident, incident, surprise, and comeuppance, strangers and oddities. We disable ourselves for the real world. No wonder THE GREAT OUTDOORS is a goner. It's just too real....

Parade Route

Parade route is supposed to be hot this season. Parade route is designated—sometimes official, often gaudy, and maybe historic—as THE place to celebrate football victories for the home team, the end of war, the homecoming of veterans, Armistice and Memorial Days, and now, the end of football season.

Parade route was the noisy venue for parades on Thanksgiving or Christmas or New Year's Day down the main drag of a college town.

That was before pro football moved into, and then was taken over by television, which expanded it into a visual freak show, new plays and players designed as much for dramatic encounter on TV as to beat the opposition.

But look now. Is the era of great and gaudy post-season parades coming to an end? Consider what happened New Year's Day in Pasadena, California. Don't tell me that tickets for the famous Parade of Roses went begging! Don't tell me the ticket scalpers themselves got scalped! Maybe it was just old stuff, a ho-hum, once-again-into-the-breach kind of game between Michigan and Washington. Or is parade route turning into just another city street?

To think the unthinkable—what happens to events like the Kentucky Derby Parade when its parade route no longer reverberates to the rumble of giant army tanks from Fort Knox? When they no longer spend our tax dollars to pay tanks and tankers to liven up parade route to celebrate a horse race? What then?

Will parade route become just further proof that, at long last, with no Russians to fight, the Cold War is really finished and done for?

PARTY STREET

Surely, Bourbon Street in the Vieux Carre of New Orleans is America's favorite PARTY STREET. And surely it's notorious for drunks, pimps, prostitutes, as well as for party goers and throwers. Surely dozens of cities now possess their very own PARTY STREET, barricaded off for homecomings, big events, conventions, and fundraisers.

But even PARTY STREET can turn ugly. When someone forgets to shut down liquor sales soon enough. Or somebody takes down the barricades and suddenly souped-up drivers try to bullhorn their way through the crowd.

Take the latest scenario in historic Georgetown in the District of Columbia. Wisconsin Avenue is Washington's premier PARTY STREET. It's a rendezvous for teenagers, where suburbanites cluster, collegians gang up, tourists stroll, pickpockets troll, and military on leave carouse. Good fun, good for business.

Until a few weeks ago. Then the party on PARTY STREET got rough. Sidewalk fistfights became street brawls. Suddenly, right there onto Wisconsin Avenue came the Rapid Deployment Unit, Washington's heavy-hitter squad organized "to target neighborhoods plagued by drugs and gun violence."[1] But there? Some other blocks in the Washington get more homicides in one year than Georgetown gets in ten.

Shopkeepers in Washington, which is, of course, the nation's finest theme park, were all a-fluster. Worried that "incidents" would hurt business. But what was at risk on Wisconsin Avenue was not life and limb, but the image of a good-time street. Nobody wanted to think...the party...might be...over.

1: "Redeployment Draws Fire: DC Police Unit Shifted to Georgetown," Brian Mooar and Keith A. Harriston, *The Washington Post*, June 7, 1992.

Party River

Party river...we explored party streets where things can get unruly on heavy-drinking weekends. Now let's consider party river. That's what I'm calling it...that place along a lazy river, in or near a city, where the current meanders, the waters are shallow, the bottom smooth, the banks accessible, and the surface is fun and games afloat—the longest socializing, beer-drinking, water-splashing and dunking party for miles around. It's an evanescent contact zone and can become a movable pickup bar, floating on impromptu rafts and lashed-together rubber inner tubes.

Every popular watercourse in temperate-zone America offers the makings of a party river: the Chattahoochee around Atlanta, the Salt River around Phoenix Arizona....

Then there's the Ocoee in North Carolina. When a rushing gush of water is released from upstream dams, it becomes what's said to be the most popular rafting river in America—for serious rafters, not party goers. Elsewhere in North Carolina they'll tell you everybody wants to get on the French Broad.

And especially there's that prime party river, the Guadeloupe of Texas. An estimated 18,000 people, often with ice chests of beer and other alcohol in tow, flock to the Guadeloupe River each weekend, and up to 30,000 on holiday weekends such as Memorial Day and Labor Days.

Kelley Shannon of the Associated Press tells us that, on the Guadeloupe, "Drunk men and women, disregarding no-trespassing signs, scale seventy-five-foot cliffs to take a river plunge." A slow-moving mass of people on inner tubes and rafts watch from the water below as a young man makes a lewd comment to a woman floating by.... Law officers rush to quell a near-riot at a popular launching spot.

Just fun-loving Texans, no doubt. But it does suggest if you take to party river any Labor Day weekend, watch out your floaters don't turn into sinkers.

Partying

We now return to PARTY STREET. No two places going by the same name could be so shockingly different as PARTY STREET. One PARTY STREET, closed off for an afternoon party, is quietly middle-class, a gathering place for the neighborhood. The big noise is the clang and clink of horseshoe games. And the roots of all this go back to the genteel ceremony of tea parties, this one preceded by invitations delivered by moms and dads oozing good manners. It ends at the appointed hour.

The other PARTY STREET starts mean at the corner and turns ugly by the next. Horseplay with liquor turns into riot. It stems from medieval street frolics and semi-barbaric routs, and, says a reporter who blundered into one last summer, it attracts "opposing currents that drink, fight, cut, scream, and growl.... Thousands of people roamed the street. Some, like us, were there out of curiosity, but most were drunk (many underage), fighting, urinating on the walls, sexually engaged, or worse.... We heard every sexual proposition known to man."

PARTY STREETS like this spring up in springtime and die back in the fall. Down at police headquarters, everybody knows where the action may be. But such PARTY STREETS never get published on official city maps. They seldom penetrate the local print media.

You, yourself, must learn to read the territory: a wet precinct adjacent to dry territory or close to a regional stadium or racetrack on Big Event Weekend.

So you learn to watch for signals: a cluster of police cars, quietly waiting; people running HARD, not playfully, across a street; angry gestures, those hand signals of violence about to surface. Such primitive signals expose the changing meanings of PARTY STREET.

Presidential Site

It began so innocently, so small scale, this proliferation of PRESIDENTIAL SITES. We want to remember that the PRESIDENTIAL SITE has become a national icon, a shrine no less. Any place that touches the office of the president or that the president touches, accumulates trappings of power that sometimes approach those of a religion.

PRESIDENTIAL SITES expand, multiply. Wherever the president moves becomes a temporary compound to be surveyed, surrounded, sealed off, and protected by the armed Secret Service—at a cost of over a million dollars a day. It's called "freezing the site." Nobody, not even members of congress, is permitted to leave for a half hour after the presidential departure.

Consider the birthplaces, the old homesteads, the Summer and Winter White Houses, the family compounds of Kennedys and Roosevelts and Bushes. Try to enumerate the sites of famous presidential visits. "George Washington slept HERE," and also THERE, and just down the road a-piece.

What about the locale of speeches, proclamations? Of press releases, sound bites, and off-the-cuff pronouncements? "Photo Opportunities" they're called. The sky's no limit: look at Air Force One, the roving PRESIDENTIAL SITE, 30,000 feet up.

Take note of the rash of new presidential centers and now nine presidential libraries—what Florida Senator Chiles called "monuments to the pharaohs." The Kennedy Library cost $21 million, The Reagan Library close to a hundred million.

The story began with 167 counties named for presidents. It's a continuing story. The naming, marking, mapping, and honoring get evangelized, as though it were indeed a new state religion. AND THE END IS NOWHERE TO BE SEEN.

Riotsville, U.S.A.

This could be the nickname of your town or mine, a name bestowed sometimes freely, but usually with caution, beginning in the 1960s. Free-floating in the lingo of those days, it came to designate any locale plagued or distinguished by frequent or large or spectacular or especially damaging riots. That was when "taking it to the streets" was a last resort for protestors over the Vietnam War or racial tensions or both.

Riotsville, U.S.A., is a loose and freely used descriptor in conversations, but unlikely to be found in local chamber of commerce publications, unless it's directed at a competing city.

As far as we can tell, the first make-believe Riotsville, U.S.A., was a training device at Fort Belvoir, Virginia, in the 1960s. According to the Associated Press, the U.S. Army "demonstrated its latest riot control tactic and equipment. The setting was 'Riotsville, U.S.A.,' a mock-up of a city swept by disorder. While about 3,000 persons observed from bleachers, a 'Riotsville' mob of soldiers dressed as hippies set fire to buildings, overturned two cars, and looted stores. Then, with bayonets fixed, troops wearing black rubber gas masks arrived on the scene and controlled the mob with tear gas."

So we may be prepared. There's always the possibility that when anything approaches a rout, a riot, an uprising, an unruly demonstration, or even a celebration turned riotous, your city or mine can be converted, in reality or by propagandistic name dropping, into Riotsville, U.S.A. It's a place-name and a place—not to be used, or dismissed, lightly.

The Setting

What we call "a SETTING" is not the cozy spot where a setting hen clucks and does her hatch work. Not at all. The modern SETTING is strictly background designed to work magic on someBODY or someTHING. It's a plausibility structure. It's a set-up, background for what is assumed to be expensive, if not elite, goings-on.

I met an ambitious executive who moved to my city to find a house before his family arrived. His wife was disgusted with what he picked—a colonial mansion with a huge verandah. "I know just what was in his cotton-pickin' mind," she told me. "He wanted to be leanin' up against that big white column with a drink in his hand when the guests got there." That is the right Old-South-Suh! SETTING. That is what a hostess wants for her Derby garden party. What ambitious Daddy will pay blood money to get for his daughter's wedding, or a chief executive, anxious for "the right atmosphere" at headquarters.

You get the picture: interior designer madly smoothing pillows in the master's suite before the photographers get there from *Architectural Digest* magazine. Great oaks framing a white-columned mansion carefully stage-set behind a nattily turned-out couple astride horses as they wait for The Hunt to start.

Here's an ad in an executive magazine: "No time, expense, materials, or workmanship were spared in transforming this secluded mountain SETTING into a retreat of incomparable beauty."[1] Some cherish all this as high adventure. I think of it as high risk—ending up with all SETTING and no substance.

1: Real estate advertisement in "The Robb Report," p 146 August 1984

THE SETUP

You know how it is when a hot rock group struts onstage in front of a screaming mob? Or when the advance crew stakes out the foundations for an $800,000 prefab, ready-to-be-assembled, six-story stage plus backdrop?

Got the picture? We're not talking impromptu stage set of sticks and canvas. We're talking THE SETUP, late model. It's not a gizmo. It's a place—the indispensable high-tech, knockdown, four-D backdrop for modern rock concerts.

Here come the tractor-trailers to line the streets. Here come platoons, if not regiments, of grips, gofers, electricians, and steelworkers. Out come the amplifiers to wake the ungrateful dead. The rock stars are chauffeured up in their stretch limos.

Over all this hoopla looms THE SETUP, a Tinker Toy six stories high. Firecrackers burst, blank-shooting cannon roar, and clouds of dry ice spread their gleaming glow. Not just for tonight. THE SETUP must survive hail and gale, riot and ruckus, knocked up and knocked down, ever-ready for the next gig stop.

The Rolling Stones' SETUP for "Starlight Express" was 300 feet high...looked like a misalliance between a shuttle launch and a North Sea oil rig...billed as the most expensive road show ever.

Did you catch the outdoor Carnival of Displaced Devotion in Seattle? It had electronic robots locked in battle, a big bone lurching and dragging itself across the stage, a "pulse-jet" sounding subsonic rumble, and an earth-digging Screw Machine.

Structures like these that travel, ramble, rumble, gargle, pose, and pout, have propelled THE SETUP into a new fourth dimension. It won't soon retreat. And as for you spacewalkers, moon rakers, planetary adventurers out there, THESE are your new role models. Don't just stand there....

Virtual Places

Before we fall away into VIRTUAL PLACES where they sell virtual reality, let me recall that memorable early day of computer reality when *Radical Software*, a tabloid magazine, introduced an early version of pre-virtual sex. The date was 1972.

Radical Software described what supposedly happened when two people, male and female, were placed fully dressed in adjoining rooms, on camera. Between them the door was shut and locked. Only if both of them used their own private combination could they get the door unlocked. It was a "consensual lock." But the two could watch each other on closed-circuit television and talk to each other by computer.

What happened next in this "new computer reality?" *Radical Software* reported that the couple, with nothing but typed words and looks to go on, achieved what was described as "a state of rapport." As surely as night follows day, this was followed by a state of arousal, at which point they consensually unlocked the door, sensually leaped into each others arms, and then—not in terms of virtual reality, but of carnal actuality—leaped into bed...off camera.

This was not, I repeat, not virtual reality, but an early foretaste of the power of second-hand experience to foretell, to simulate, or to stimulate The Real Thing.

"There is something about...virtual reality that sends people's thoughts drifting in the general direction of sex," said Robert Wright in the *Los Angeles Times*. You get his drift. Put on this new multi-vision headgear; immerse yourself electronically in virtual reality; and you too, as they say, can have it all.

I doubt it. From my one slight test run into pre-virtual reality—not much more than a set-up display of holograms—I concluded that electronic places are still fuzz and buzz. Some of its promoters suggest that you get yourself an electronic buzz, self-stimulate sexual or other fantasies, and you'll convince yourself it's The Real Thing. But if you believe that, you'll believe anything.

WRECK SITE

WRECK SITE...there's always a question as to where the wreck actually took place, legally speaking, that is. Was it the moment of impact when the gyrating wingtip of a plane out of control clipped the treetops?

Was it that quarter mile of broken trees and flayed aluminum bits of Cessna or Piper or Hellcat scattered through the woods or exploded on the desert? Did it extend off the highway, where they're still prizing corpses out of cars locked in heavy metal embrace?

After the wreck is over, WRECK SITE attracts scavengers, lawyers, wreckers, and the new breed of forensic specialists who, as expert witnesses, testify for and against insurance companies. Here come kinfolk, here come survivors who try to put up white crosses to mark the deadly WRECK SITE.

Highway police, traffic experts, and observant travelers learn to spot WRECK SITES—places for accidents waiting to happen...that Dead Man's Curve a half mile past the midnight heavy drinkers' watering hole. And they watch out for that remote, four-way highway intersection with a downhill run from two directions to beat the stoplight...another WRECK SITE, for sure!

Traces left behind at WRECK SITE may differ as much as the testimony of eye witnesses. The largest WRECK SITE of our times lies in the Gulf Stream off Cape Kennedy in Florida where the Challenger spacecraft exploded. The fields of debris on the bottom of the Atlantic Ocean covered an extent of 480 square miles.

That is the size of a modern WRECK SITE. It foreshadows the new generation WRECK SITE across the battle zones, land and sea, in and around the Persian Gulf, and whatever may follow.

Transitions 4

FALL COLOR COUNTRY

It happens about this time every year—that sudden intrusion of the passing throng, city life, the great world at large—into my private garden. Into MY little refuge, MY sequestered and somewhat intimate backyard. It's been a world of my own where I can dig and delve, pick and prune, and—communing with nature—watch my garden grow.

All of a sudden, just in a few days, my protective screen of vegetation began to fritter and fray away with the autumn leaves. The privacy that came with summer leaves is gone with the autumn breeze. My vegetative surround of green and gold has gradually shriveled and shrunk.

Through days of early fall that quickly passed, I was safely tucked away behind the protective screen of FALL COLOR COUNTRY. But the leaves that hid me and my work from the passing parade have turned gold and red and brown, and now sprawl dead and fallen across the garden. They will not blow away. I must cart them off to the compost pile.

When I look up from my labors, not only do I hear the passing traffic—I SEE it. My garden is no longer exclusively mine. Thanks to the falling leaves, it's now part of somebody else's view, part of THEIR passing scene, THEIR roadside, a local sight for THEM to enjoy and take away with them. My garden!

On second thought, maybe I should consider the view as part of my surplus garden produce—more than I can use, another crop to be given away freely for others to enjoy.

At least, that's what I keep telling myself, now that I've "gone public for the winter" and become part of the view.

HURRICANE PATH

Deep down within the sinuous swirl of an eddy of moist air, somewhere offshore to the south, a tropical hurricane is born. Nobody can predict the spot. But, who knows? This year is what's called a "good hurricane year." West Africa's had a wet season. For the Caribbean that generally means hurricanes, which usually run in cycles. The experts say our so-called "current peaceful cycle" may be ending.

This year's hurricane season began June first and runs through November. That's official. If you get hit by one, it was done legally and on schedule. You have been warned.

Not only that, but The Big One is overdue. Suppose we do get a Big One in '92, like Hugo that hit the Carolinas in '89. Hugo killed twenty-nine people, did six-billion dollars of damage to South Carolina alone. If The Big One hits Miami or New Orleans, it could do damage in the scores of billions. Kill a thousand or so people. Two such storms could play havoc with the insurance industry. We have all been warned.

Not that most of us take notice. A surprising number of people, even smack in HURRICANE PATH, think it smart, or "with it" to be nonchalant, unflappable, unconcerned.

Well, the other day a batch of hurricane experts got together at Coral Gables. That's a multi-billion-dollar stumble along the next or later HURRICANE PATH. The experts took grim notice of the forty million people who have moved into HURRICANE PATHS along the American coastline. Most, over eighty per cent, have never lived through a major hurricane. Many won't live through the next Big One. Sorry about that. Maybe we all need a good map of HURRICANE PATH...tattooed on our foreheads.

My Hurricane

It was a hurricane that had no name...back in the pre-christening era before they gave girls' names, and then boys' names, to tropical hurricanes off the southern coast.

That was when I was a kid, evacuated from Saint Simons Island off the Georgia coast. The day before the hurricane-that-had-no-name struck, we played the game of double dare with giant ten-foot waves, down on the beach. But the Coast Guard woke us up at 2 A.M. and rousted us out and we refugeed off to the mainland in the dark. Sloshed through seawater hub-deep around our car. When it was over, our house stood undamaged.

Later we learned this was only the twitch at the tail end of the hurricane that emptied out the waters of Lake Okeechobee down in Florida and killed 1,836 people.

That was before the resort boom and the second-home boom hit the Atlantic and Gulf coastlines. Since then, some twenty million or more Americans have moved into hurricane paths... built homes—and what they thought were futures—in the most hurricane/high-water/sea-surge/tornado-and-looting-prone parts of the United States.

Scratch a coastal county and you've got a growth area smack in a prospective hurricane path.

This week thousands of homes built since the last hurricane were smashed or damaged when Hurricane Andrew hit Florida and Louisiana. Thanks to radar, radio, and television, most people got the message and refugeed out. But at least fifteen billion dollars of damage stayed behind. And hurricane paths stay behind.

Chances are, the same pressures that failed to stop people from building in hurricane paths will soon be prompting them to rebuild in hurricane paths to get ready for the next big blow.

THE ICE

THE ICE: a place touted by high-tech tacticians as yet another new frontier.

Given proper latitude and altitude, THE ICE is inevitable—lots of it in glaciers, continents full of it at the poles. Or a glass of it—make that "whiskey and a splash."

Natural ice occurs at that meeting place between life in suspension and life in action. In all water lies the possibility of ice. And all ice can melt down to water. Each is in a permanent state of pure potential.

What else takes so many forms? Through thick and thin... mushy, greasy, oily, wavy?... It's deceptively passive. It gives you a place to stand...on the ocean. As a broken pack in the sea-lanes, it's a threat to ships. When it lies flat, smooth, and frigid, it's all speed and mobility for skaters, iceboaters, dogsledders. Ask any Eskimo, Aleut, Outer Mongolian, or other extreme latitudinarian. They'll tell you...hard ice means fast moves across big space.

On top of THE ICE the high-technicians are building artificial-ice islands for drilling equipment. Ambitious shippers—with the world's biggest icebreaker ships—want to break THE ICE on the Great Lakes for shipping all winter long! High-tech hunters, with ice-breaking-and-entering tools, peek under THE ICE and see fish to catch, minerals on the bottom, and below that—petroleum.

You can find hunting and harvest seasons year-round on THE ICE. It's slippery territory in transition from geographic place to world commodity, up for grabs.

MEETING PLACE

It's just a simple agreement between friends. It goes like this: GOTCHA. I'LL GETCHA. SEEYA. Which, of course, translates "I understand. I will come and get you. So long till then."

But something's left out of this GOTCHA-GETCHA-SEEYA. And that's MEETCHA—which is the exact MEETING PLACE where I'm gonna SEEYA.

It could be as simple as YOUR PLACE or MY PLACE, but if I'm gonna GETCHA someplace else, that's a horse on a different track. And it won't do to say, "You can't miss it."

Back in the mid-century, "Amos 'n Andy," a radio comedy team, had a MEETCHA routine. It went like this: "I'll MEETCHA at the corner. If you get there first, you make a chalk mark on the light post. If I get there first, I'll rub it out."

Among thousands of east coast collegians of the first George Bush and later generations, a favorite weekend MEETCHA place for Ivy Leaguers was "under the clock at The Biltmore," a Manhattan hotel in New York City.

By the 1980s, thousands of eager beavers had moved into the MEETCHA business, manufacturing hundreds of look-alike airports, convention centers, resorts, restaurant-bars-with-volleyball, and other meeting places with no distinct place to MEETCHA: every place looked like someplace else.

And so today you find that ubiquitous but mundane solution: the big indoor signboard that says MEETING PLACE. GOTCHA, GETCHA, SEEYA, MEETCHA.

Nonfarm Farms

Over the past year I've been traveling stretches of that great old national road, U.S. 40, across the middle of the American heartland. It was built in the early 1800s to open up The West—from Cumberland, Maryland, westward. And it passes through Wheeling, West Virginia; Columbus, Ohio; Terre Haute, and Indianapolis, on its way to St. Louis, Missouri. It was on this road that my companions and I encountered the NONFARM FARM.

Some people call these affairs "HOBBY FARMS, RETIREMENT FARMS, PART-TIME FARMS." But "NONFARM FARM" tells you best what's going on...which is to say: Not! Very! Much! in the way of actual, honest-to-God dirt farming.

How can you tell a NONFARM FARM from the road? With interpretation by my geographer companion, Professor Karl Raitz, I can summon up the evidence that came pouring off the roadside. There are broad green fields, but no animals, no feeding cattle. The barn looks empty. The buildings are all painted the same white-white, apparently at the same-same time.

The silo is obsolete. There's no heavy farm machinery in sight. Standing near the house is a horse trailer. Aha! A saddle horse trailer to take around to horse shows...a hobbyhorse!

Grass has moved into the barn lot; it's no longer trampled bare. In fact, there are NO deep, muddy ruts, or mud tracked in from the fields.

The air is filled with the natural aroma of fresh-mown grass—AND the acrid smell of herbicides. Not fresh-mown hay, but city-type lawn grass.

There's a compulsive, suburban neatness about the whole place.

And that's the story of the great old national road. Once it connected working farms to the market—once part of the great American food-production line. Now it's just another link in the chain of consumption.

Presence

What is this thing called "PRESENCE"? Is it no more than a mythical aura surrounding a famous person? Actually, PRESENCE is a hot word in geopolitics. The United States now has a substantial PRESENCE in the Middle East. Japan's automobile plants give it a PRESENCE in the United States

PRESENCE, though it may not actually define "territory," suggests power even when it doesn't yet exercise it. Always in the offing is the possibility of armed enforcement of outside rules or intervention by outsiders.

We got our answer in the Persian Gulf War. The United States' PRESENCE in the Middle East, it turned out, consisted of the physical, geographical reality of docks and refueling stations, of air and ground military bases, of observations posts, command posts, minefields, defensive perimeters, staging areas. It consisted of fleet anchorages, listening stations and antenna farms, of supply depots, lines of communication, fallback positions, and debarcation zones.

Get all these places together in one part of the world and you have one powerful PRESENCE indeed!

It's clear that PRESENCE has moved out of geopolitics and gone local. We read in a headline that "Federal Presence in Alabama Town Helps Cut Crime, Police Chief Says." PRESENCE is now local: evidence of distant, ever-expanding authority, chiefly by the federal government. Look around. The federal PRESENCE may be closer than you thought!

The Scene

Scene, the...in today's lingo, is not something you merely view, but something you "make." And the scene you construct is a complex demonstration area of short duration and extended notoriety. The scene is designed to make or break reputations.

The scene requires an economic base—a leisure class with excess cash; one that is courted, full-time, by hustling, ambitious, table-hopping, publicity-seeking wanna-be groupies, agents, social climbers, artists, costumiers, actors, and hangers-on trying to outdo, out-glitter, out-con each other in making the scene.

None of which is to be confused with the socially unacceptable act of "making a scene," or creating a gross disturbance that calls out the cops. Not at all. Making the scene consists, in part, of organizing or contriving a particular stage setting, but also of being seen, quoted, photographed, and remembered as having been there in the company of others more famous or notorious.

Remember Rick's Bar in the movie "Casablanca"? Now that was the scene! Today's most notorious scenes are in Manhattan, Toronto, London, Paris...Los Angeles is moving up. Such world cities have got the apparatus.

Scene makers need TV—TV—TV shows, gossip columnists out-whispering or out-shouting each other. "Downtown magazines" rising and falling with waves of gainful publicity. For scene sniffers, "making it" is a full-time occupation. This is where rewards go to the quick-with-a-quip, to the outrageous and obstreperous, specialists in staying just ahead of the law of diminishing returns.

MAKING THE SCENE

It's time to take a second look at THE SCENE. There are, one man says, "no sirens, no bullhorns, and no protests, but only the sound of thousands of doors shutting quietly...as Americans turn their backs on 'THE SCENE'."

What an evocative sound, what an image: "doors shutting quietly...Americans turning their backs..."

And what are they door-shutting, back-turning AGAINST? Against THE SCENE? Against goings-on in public? Against life in the public realm and domain? Against the great American encounter zone—everybody's school yard—that place we call "in public"?

Such avoidance of reality, such a purported presumable trend, such looking the other way, is called "digging in." Those quotes above are from Shanna Nix, a writer for the *San Francisco Chronicle*, who says digging in is a "rejection of THE SCENE for more private pursuits."

That's also what the man says digging in is all about. But I say it's a way to say "Stop the world, I want to get off." It's slow death by shrivel and shrink; it's copping out by bugging off; it's getting away from it all; staying shut-in and saying to hell with the Great Out There. It's a script of whine and whimper, a Trip-Tik of retreat...a shrug expanded into a lifestyle.

If we all dig in and bug out, who's left to people the streets, throng the sidewalks, stroll the alleys, rally to causes one-on-one, to learn the body English of life-in-company?

Enough of that digging in, I say. Leave it to the cop-outs, I say. The rest of us need to learn the ropes, to hustle the bustle, agree to disagree, master repartee, and enjoy the give-and-take of life out in society, out in the open, out in the public domain, in THE SCENE. That's what I call making, not dropping out of— THE SCENE!

TWILIGHT ZONE

What IS there about TWILIGHT ZONE that attracts and nurtures characters and creatures, who and which are often beyond the pale, and denizens of two worlds?

TWILIGHT ZONE can denote a neighborhood occupied by social hangers-on or a disputed workplace between two labor unions or a potential drug scene on a seldom-policed and dimly-lit street. Or a neighborhood frequented—but how can you be sure—by refugees from assorted classes or ethnic groups in an odd mixture.

So powerful has been the influence of a Rod Stirling TV drama called "The TWILIGHT ZONE" that the name itself has acquired an aura of being almost, but not quite, beyond the touch or taint— a science fiction version—of reality.

TWILIGHT ZONE has migrated, along with its obscurities, into sociology and common usage, each of which picks its way between This-ness and That-ness.

But how did TWILIGHT ZONE get seized by negative connotation along the way? Was it the absence of The Light, or the presence of The Dark, that made TWILIGHT ZONE a place to avoid?

By itself, the word ZONE picks up bad vibes from seedy company. The Dictionary of Sociology says it's a place "…in a temporary state of deterioration characterized by a lower grade land use than formerly, and not yet ripe for succeeding more valuable land use." The expression "changing neighborhood" slinks along under the same assumption—any change is bound to be for the worse.

And so I'm tempted to conclude that TWILIGHT ZONE is any place so deprived of daylight or human understanding as to offer partial truth in place of the real thing—a good place for duck hunters, frog-giggers, runaways, and social climbers. Hang in there!

THE START

For sporting events, THE START is preordained. It's well marked for marathons, parades, and other goings-on that use public rights-of-way. Once upon a time THE START of a race was a simple affair—perhaps a white string held taut by teammates at a high school 100-yard dash.

But specialists wouldn't leave THE START alone. They made it complex, gave it more space. They added official observers, stands for photographers, and space for fans who pay extra to be at THE START.

Look at the Indy 500 on Memorial Day. The ritual begins with "Gentlemen, start your engines!" Race car drivers maneuver into the starting grid and cross THE START in a pecking order that turns into a free-for-all frenzy.

In horse racing THE STARTing gate is a complex and mobile contraption wheeled into place for each race. Easy to see, fun to watch, all recorded for TV and posterity.

But off track, out in the real world, precisely where things began is a matter of endless debate among historians, courtroom witnesses, patriotic zealots, and participants in a street fight.

Did World War I really start at the street assassination of the Archduke Ferdinand of Serbia and his wife in Sarajevo, capital of Bosnia-Herzegovina? Didn't the American Civil War actually start long before the bombardment of Fort Sumter, in South Carolina? And will you please tell the court exactly where you were standing when you saw the defendant starting to shoot?

To what point in time, to what place, will surviving historians be pointing when they try to sort out THE STARTing place of World War III?

THE WET

Once upon a time everybody knew what you meant when you said "THE WET." It was an all-too-familiar place, not just a condition.

Everybody in the eastern American states encountered bogs, wetwoods, marshes, swamps, muck and mire, inundation lands, bottomlands, wet prairie, and miasma land. Louisville once had so much miasma land, a 19th century term for mosquitoey wetwoods, it was known as "The Graveyard of the West."

So early Americans took the usual defensive step—they mobilized the English language against THE WET. They talked—in a source I've misplaced—about "eerie nighttime wastelands…bogs of treachery, mires of despair, homes of pests, and refuges for outlaw and rebel."

By the 1850s, Americans assumed a God-given, if not constitutional, right to dry land. That was the year the feds gave the states sixty-four-million acres of so-called "swampland." It was supposedly unfit for cultivation. But lots of it turned out to be high and dry. Speculators, who had helped write the new law, made a killing on selling it off.

I like to define "THE WET" by backing into it. A city is a huge pump for drying out and drying up THE WET. I have said, perhaps too often, "Urbanization equals desiccation." If city folks suck up and pump out hard enough, they can dry out THE WET several counties away—and destroy the habitats of millions of plants and wild animals.

By the middle of the last century, draining THE WET had become a national obsession. Doing it by hook, crook, or thievery was widespread. And so it turns out today that our latest endangered species of place is THE WET.

The South—What's Left

Every time I go SOUTH—at least once a year into THE DEEP SOUTH and every few weeks to someplace south of where I'm writing and speaking—I ask myself "How can you tell when you get there, to the real SOUTH?"

"Well," said my friend, "YOU ought to know; you've been traveling back and forth all your life." But when I start listing what is it?—what are the visible outdoor signs that say, "You have arrived in THE SOUTH?"—funny things happen on the way to an answer.

First, as you go south, it warms up. If you start in late wintertime, a hard day's drive takes you into spring. Magnolia in full bloom, Spanish moss in full droop, the out-of-doors greening up. And it's not so citified. It's got huge, open, endless stretches of well-vegetated countryside that distinguish THE SOUTH.

It's at least 500 vegetated miles between metropolitan cities. There is no southern mega-city (Atlanta is top candidate), no hundred-mile city, no East Coast megalopolis like that eight-hundred-mile city between Boston and Washington, D.C.

The closest southern candidate beyond Atlanta is the so-called "Piedmont Crescent" of North Carolina that takes in Charlotte-Greensboro-Chapel Hill-Raleigh-Durham. But it's a small, which is to say a southern, version of the real thing up north.

Third, THE SOUTH still has the nation's biggest collection of dilapidated, worn-out, broken-down, freestanding structures: old tenant shacks, abandoned farmhouses, decrepit barns and cotton gins. Run-down backwoods cabins, falling-down fences, unpainted outbuildings, and vacated storefronts and empty filling stations alongside the old highways.

Fourth, THE SOUTH is still a great source of raw materials piled-up and being shipped out: logs and timber, trees and lumber, oranges, grapefruit, vegetables, catfish, what's left of Gulf Coast shrimp, all to be processed up north. On occasion, you find signs of that perennial place called "THE NEW SOUTH" but it seems to consist—I hope I am wrong—mostly of mass-produced roadside strips.

Still and all, Southerners are making endless new starts and restarts at small-budget, outdoor enterprises: baby golf courses; family farm-restaurants; roadside barbecues; Mom and Pop Roadside Multiple Enterprise Zones; drive-in, pick-up points never touched by ice or snow; yard sales; junk barns; roller rinks; and rinkey-dinks in endless outdoor profusion.

Destinations 5

Destinations

That's where we're all going. Someplace. Nobody moves just to
be moving. Even people going around the track, around the block,
using up gas, taking up time…they're all going someplace. Call it
around, call it a target, call it goal, a rest stop, over to Joe's Video.
Call it DESTINATION—or even destiny.

To get there from here, to arrive at somewhere else, you've still
got to go someplace and stop someplace. It may turn out to be a
restaurant called "Someplace Else," or a corner bar called "The
Other Place." Every trip needs a DESTINATION, even if you're only
cruising, joyriding, bugging-out, or doing that indefinable,
undecipherable thing called "making the scene."

Because what you're passing through out there, what we're
all part of out there, like it or not, is a goal-oriented society,
watching to see where you're going. Everyplace is a place to go, a
place to stop, pause, and reconsider, a place for making, buying,
selling, negotiating; a point of no return, a DESTINATION. And if
you've really and truly got no place to go, you are—I don't need
to tell you—in deep trouble.

If somebody tells you, "You got no place to go but out," that's
a challenge or an insult. If somebody asks you, "Where are you
from?" that's looking backward to yesterdays maybe better left
forgotten. And, maybe none of your business, Buster!

But to ask, "Where are you going?"—that's exploratory,
anticipatory, forward-looking. And even if, by chance, you are
actually going no place at all, getting there may be more than half
the fun. I do hope you make it….

Abandoned Farms

Out here at the edge of town lie the ABANDONED FARMS…. The tip of the iceberg, reminders of abandonment all over North America…. The hopes and fears of all the years gathered right in sight. The ABANDONED FARM house doors flap in the wind. Tree limbs fall on the slant-roof porch. No dogs bark, no cows moo and need milking, no mail for the sagging mailbox….

Real dirt farmers at the edge of town have few incentives to keep farming. Suburban kids and dogs damage livestock and fences. Even with tax abatements for the so-called "working farm," expenses mount up.

There's many a tale to tell, and sometimes capital gains to split up. Look at this farm: the old folks are dead and the young'uns wrangle in court over the will. Here's another…. You can barely see it since Old MacDonald sold off the frontage for houses. Look yonder: an old eyesore, yes it was. A developer bought it at the courthouse door, is holding it for better times.

These ABANDONED FARMS come in waves. After the Erie Canal opened up The West, New England farmers quit their rocky hillsides by the thousands and moved out and away. In every depression people quit farming.

But depressions cut both ways at the edge of town. Many banks quit staking house builders to new projects on old farms. Some environmental protection slows down the filling up of wetlands, the cutting down of forests.

The next ABANDONED FARM you see at the edge of town, take a hard look. It may show which way the economic winds do blow.

Arrival Zone

You won't find this on the map, along with other non-existent-but-wouldn't-they-be-wonderful places called "the entrance to the city, city gateway," or "the overlook station."

This is the place which millions of travelers and visitors know and cherish—that spot on the highway where you catch your very first glimpse of your destination: the town or city that lies just ahead, just on or over the horizon, beyond the next hill. You can't wait to get there.

It's that sudden breathtaking view of Manhattan as you come down off the New Jersey palisades. It's that dramatic glimpse of San Francisco from the expressway near Candlestick Park; of Jacksonville or Tampa or Norfolk or Madison, Indiana, from their tall river- or bay-crossing bridges; of Cincinnati from the great cut of Interstate 71 coming down off Kentucky's high ground; or the "you-hafta-watch-to-see-it" view of Louisville's skyline from Interstate 65 coming south, or 64 coming west.

It makes you want to pull off the highway—right there—and get out; take time to see where you're going; check the map; get a free-for-visitors computer printout to show how to get there, to tell you what's going on there.

But that's still a traveler's pipe dream. Without such well-equipped ARRIVAL ZONES, getting there is a matter of blind luck, or blindly following interstates, or super-careful attention to fluttering maps on the car seat.

But doing anything blindly on highways is a danger to life, limb, and your insurance policy. Sorry folks, many an ARRIVAL ZONE is still a place you can't get to from here.

The Big World

"It's a BIG WORLD out there." That's the way preachers begin, the way sermons start, the way warnings get going. THE BIG WORLD is a threat to those of us who are not big, not worldly, and by implication are stuck back here, unprepared for life out there in THE BIG WORLD.

How big is THE BIG WORLD? We might say, "It's as big as all outdoors." Or that it "goes from here to eternity." Or we try to pull it down to human scale when we say, "The world's his oyster" or "she made it out in THE BIG WORLD."

But the fact is, THE BIG WORLD is whatever is out there, and that's quite a roomy, cosmic dimension beyond most folks' reach, presence, vision, experience, or kinship system.

THE BIG WORLD makes itself felt at the point where here comes to a stop. It is that bigger part of that more threatening place called "out there." The key thing about THE BIG WORLD is that there's nothing small, intimate, graspable, negotiable; nothing down-to-earth, just-us-folksy about it.

It's populated by more than two billion people, only a smidgen of a fraction of whom we will ever know, not to mention the 3.2 more billion strangers who will be added by the year 2020— an increase of sixty percent in the population out there.

So we better stop thinking of them as strangers, foreigners, competitors, and realize we're all right here together in the same boat. It's a big leap, but they in THE BIG WORLD will outnumber us back here about two million to one!

The Boondocks

So, here we are, out in THE BOONDOCKS, also known as "the sticks, the bush, the back forty, the outback, williwags, Siberia." And also "hell and gone."

THE BOONDOCKS probably entered mainland American English as a generic man-made place around 1910, brought back by army veterans from the insurrection in the Philippines. The name comes from Tagalog, the word "B-U-N-D-O-K" meaning "rough country," the interior behind jagged mountains and inaccessible to Americans.

Later, in the 1930s, American sailors came back from Pacific duty talking, not too openly, about a district of whorehouses known as THE BOONDOCKS located, not too inaccessibly, in Shanghai. The word came back en masse with American troops returning from World War II.

More recently, American writer William Least Heat Moon set out to write a book about "the three million miles of bent and narrow rural American two-lane, the roads to Podunk and Toonerville. Into the sticks, the boondocks, the burgs, backwaters, jerkwaters, the wide spots in the road…the middle of nowhere."

By the 1960s weather casters were predicting weather "out in THE BOONIES." It became a favorite term for headline writers to deal with any scene beyond their ken or below their own horizons.

Let's face it, THE BOONDOCKS are always distant from whoever uses the term. It's city dwellers' slang to locate, if not to denigrate, the non-city. So we leave THE BOONDOCKS lurking out there, somewhere beyond the pale, another colorful trophy piggybacked home from the wars that Americans go overseas to fight.

Casinos

They're landing whoppers down on Water Street, suckers on Dock Street, keepers on Front Street. Lots of folks seem to be angling for the big one that got away—not a fish, but a five-story-tall riverboat gambling CASINO.

That's the talk, down at the town landings along the Ohio, the Wabash, and the Mississippi and Missouri Rivers, when they're not obsessed with recouping losses from the Great Flood. On the un-flooded waterfronts, the big deal is gambling. The hot locations are dockside.

Non-betters should be aware that the number of slot machines on the riverfronts of Mississippi doubled in one month and that gambling has moved up front into everyday language. A gambling CASINO is described as "a Godsend," which must come as a shock to ministers who see gambling as the Devil's handiwork.

While God and the Devil compete for Kentucky, legalized gambling flourishes on horse races—but not on riverboats.

Elsewhere on the Ohio River, gambling is said to have established a beachhead with the maiden voyage out of Metropolis, Illinois, of a glitzy, seven-million-dollar, three-story Players' Riverboat CASINO. It can make five trips a day, carry 1,400 people, and hopes to extract fifty-two dollars from each and every one.

Illinois has licensed six boats; nine will be operating within a year. Gambling river boating has yet to establish its own argot, or special slang; most of its expressions migrate, like its customers, off of dry land.

To "take a bath" on a riverboat casino means you lost your shirt, not that you got wet. When riverboat gamblers "land a big one," it's that heavy hitter who staggers up the gangplank and "makes waves" by reckless betting. They don't hoist anchor; they heist it.

Drop Zone

When we say "DROP ZONE" we're not talking air-to-ground combat. And it's not just the military zone where paratroopers and supplies get dropped from planes in combat. We're talking civilian talk, and you won't find this kind of DROP ZONE on your handy-dandy city map.

DROP ZONE is a geographic term, supplied for this venue by a Chicago city planner, William Knack. It's a zone of transition, where land values and productive human activities drop off or diminish. It's often called "a declining area, zone of transition, or zone of discard."

Several DROP ZONES may coexist as non-growth rings around a city center. In such places, would-be dumpers feel free to drop their trash. Other would-be dumpers follow their example. At DROP ZONE, car thieves feel more secure in break-ins; fly-by-night repairmen get away with shoddy work when city inspectors close their eyes to goings-on in DROP ZONES. Closer scrutiny of DROP ZONE shows it often doubles as a refuge of poor minorities, homeless, and other city folks whose defenses are down.

You needn't be a sociologist to spot DROP ZONE. Just stop your car at the end of the off ramp the next time you exit a local expressway. Roll down your left-hand window. Look down at the gutter. It's full of cigarette butts, right? It's where careless slobs, impatiently waiting for the light to change, open their left-hand doors and empty out their dashboard ashtrays into the gutter, right? That is your neighborhood DROP ZONE.

FIRE TOWER

Far up on top of this rickety, steel, wind-whistling, old, abandoned FIRE TOWER, high up on a knobby hilltop twenty miles distant from my hometown, there are no fires to watch for, no fire warden-and-watcher, no binoculars, no wind gauges. There's only me…looking at my hometown nestled down in a faraway valley by the great river. It's a big city, but from a fire tower twenty miles up in the hills, its few skyscrapers barely stick up into my altitude.

This is a good spot to watch a city. It reminds we city folks that—for all our presence and pretensions, for all our domination of business, politics, and television—here in the Great Out There, here in the boondocks, is where it all began and begins.

Here, and not downtown, is where the oxygen we breathe is generated from earth processes and plant life. Here, and not in suburbia, is where trees grow into forests, into lumber, into two-by-sixes, into ceiling joists, into housing.

I look out over rich farmland in the valleys. Here is where corn grows and gets chopped up into silage to fill the silos, feed the cattle that supply the slaughterhouses and hamburgers that magnetize the drive-in trade.

Down there, my city neighbors like to say the city is the Engine of Civilization. But they forget that from up here in the FIRE TOWER, the city is an interruption to the spread-out world of field and forest and spring and streams…where life begins, and without which there would be no food, no supplies, no cities.

GATHERING PLACE

I started this trip thinking about the GATHERING PLACE, that place with a Biblical sound to it, the down-by-the-riverside kind of place where Moses hid, where Pharaoh's army got drowned. Where Jesus spoke, and the multitudes gathered and the loaves and the fishes appeared. And the people were fed.

But those aren't the only GATHERING PLACES that speak to our needs today. For in the here and now we need GATHERING PLACES as experimental labs for an open society, testing grounds for friendships, for ideas, for opinions—where you can let it all hang out, without getting hung up in anger, or otherwise hung for subversive ideas.

In the true GATHERING PLACE, there are no subversive ideas. Anything goes. Let men and women say their piece. Keep the peace, keep open space for hard-liners, one liners, party liners, and folks with no line at all.

But if we let GATHERING PLACES get dominated by ignorant toughs shouting down a president or building walls and fences or itching to be gunmen rather than sportsmen, then GATHERING PLACES are done in, put out, cast off, and society is the worse for it.

Democratic societies need all the GATHERING PLACES we can develop...training grounds where you learn how to get along in public. It's called civility. When people come to talk and then begin to shout, it's a place to keep the peace, hear them out, not shout them down. That's what GATHERING PLACE is all about.

HIDEAWAYS

You won't find it marked on the calendar, and you won't see a billboard proclaiming, "It's over." But what we have been going through, these last hot weeks of summer, is the closing down of the building season for HIDEAWAYS.

Did they set new building records, was the construction index up or down? I really can't tell you. And they don't really care—the kids who build HIDEAWAYS.

These go by many names: forts, hideouts, castles, interplanetary headquarters, tree houses, shacks, secret places, clubs, or simply Our Place—You Keep Out. These are those tiny constructions made by kids on vacation from schools.

Kids' HIDEAWAYS do not front on the public right-of-way; they do not have street or lot numbers, that is, they have no addresses at all. They're in the outback, nestled in the odd lots, the dells and ditches and dingles that somehow escape the platitudes of subdivision latitude and longitude.

They're not easy to locate, for kids naturally seep into nooks and crannies that don't fit the mental maps of grown-ups.

They don't need or get building permits and a change of zoning. Rather, they occupy untaxed, unnumbered, leftovers from the last building boom, odd bits and stitches in the city fabric.

If kids are lucky, they grow up in neighborhoods full of odd and neat and secret places to build HIDEAWAYS, and in neighborhoods where it's safe to be in a HIDEAWAY, where a getaway route is not a matter of life and death.

Soon enough, fall will come, trees will shed leaves, tall grasses will collapse, and HIDEAWAYS will be exposed to public view. Theirs is a summer thing. They don't winter well. So, until the next building season, "see you later alligator," or whatever turns out to be the password to next spring's new batch of HIDEAWAYS.

Light Saving

If you go outdoors after supper on November first and discover that you are still in that place called "the light," you will be caught up in the ancient ritual of daylight worship.

First, you need to remember that Daylight Saving Time, formerly known as "Summer Time," comes to an end at midnight, October 31. Then reset your clocks one hour back, by the rule: "Spring Forward, Fall Back."

Turning the clock back, take a moment to recall the remarkable man whose hand guides your hands on the clock. He was William Willett, the man who invented Daylight Saving Time.

Mr. Willett was an English contractor in London who became a millionaire builder of mansions for other millionaires. He noticed that in the spring when he took his 6:30AM horseback ride, the spring sun was up and shining brightly, but most houses still had blinds closed tightly, shutters shut, people still asleep. And in the fall as days grew short and daylight diminished, accidents among his workmen increased.

So in 1907 he published a pamphlet entitled, "The Waste of Daylight." He advocated that clocks change with the sun to pick up that extra hour of sunlight and cut down the cost of artificial lighting and on-the-job accidents.

Mr. Willett died in the middle of World War I, disappointed that his idea for a special Summer Time had not caught on. But a brash young politician brought the idea before Parliament. The light dawned, the bill passed in 1916, and Daylight Saving Time spread from England 'round the world.

Today, Willett, Limited, still exists in the building business in England. As the politician who introduced the bill said, Mr. Willett deserved "one of the finest epitaphs that any man could win—he gave more light to his countrymen."

That politician was Winston Churchill. So you may thank him and Mr. William Willett when you come to the end of our latest daylight-saving season.

Nostalgia Farm

You see 'em, strung out on highways and byways, proclaiming their presence with cutesy, folksy, artsy-crafty whimsy, loosey-goosey-gander pandering to all the nostalgia let loose in the land when the last, real, honest-to-God dirt farm on this highway disappeared down yonder-way.

This is the new NOSTALGIA FARM. You pass 'em, down at the crossroads, out by the interchange. Billboards entice you to take a trip Down Home, Back on the Farm, brunch at the Mom and Pop Homestead. Just like it usta be? With a parking lot for 500 cars? Oversize slots for tour buses from Big City?

Welcome to NOSTALGIA FARM, the made-over model for leaf watchers in the fall, sleigh riders at the first snow. Welcome to the Welcome Wagon out front, where you sign in and sign up for pick-your-own pumpkins, and, if you'da come a few weeks sooner, you'da been pulling-your-own sweet corn on your own sweet time.

Welcome to NOSTALGIA FARM...where Old MacDonald picked up ideas from the new MacDonald's—and sells...atmosphere: Smell the pigs! Don't step in the poke. Sniff the cow! Pet the goat! Stroke the shoat! Pick the pumpkin! No, put that one back, it's too big!

Spend time and money at NOSTALGIA FARM. It's the latest "transitional-land-use," as they call it down at the Tax Assessor's Office. And at the next Zoning Commission meeting, the neighbors will say: "Next thing you know, Old MacDonald will want a shopping center...." Welcome to NOSTALGIA FARM.

Out Back

Out back is a roomy package, a big umbrella, a signpost, and a destination. All this and more. Out back is where we put things we don't want up front. Out back is where we consign goings-on that we want to hide, can't move easily, or want handy, but not up too close.

Consider what we put out back. Dogs and kids, to begin with, close to the kitchen. Inside the fence that you can't put around the front yard. Utilities, for another: poles, wires, transformers, and repair trucks. Old stuff we don't want to throw away. So it goes, not in the front yard, not in the crowded basement, not in the no-longer-existent stable but...out back.

Out back has a long history. It was where the plantation owners put their slave houses. It was where Great Grandpa put the privy, the stable, and the pile of manure. It was where the servants lived—over the garage, out back. Where minority groups are sequestered still today.

But up front simply can't get along without an out back. Each depends on the other. In fact, we can't get along without knowing front from back; it's a basic fact of knowing one's place in the world. We see what's up front while out back remains invisible. Front is positive, visible, good. Back is negative, invisible, difficult.

Is it any wonder, then, that in Australia the whole vast interior of that continent—distant, far-removed, thinly populated—is called "the outback"? And that term is moving into American usage—the ultimate put-down used by everybody who wants to live up front.

OUT THERE

"Out" barges into life in many forms and guises…as in out-of-bounds, out of town, out of state, Out West, out-of-the-way, out of reach. It can leave us out of breath, out of cash, out of touch, and out of sorts.

Whether you are in or out is determined by the view from the center. If you get OUT of touch, or OUT of reach, or OUT of your gourd, you're plainly OUT of it—out of the center of things.

Westbrook Pegler, that eternally angry columnist, had a term for uppity words he didn't like. He called them "OUT-of-town words."

If we think we occupy the center of the universe, everything else is OUT THERE. Who decides what's in and what's out? Why, of course, the so-called "We" who decide things, generally in the center of things.

It's been like that. Places like downtown, the heart of the city, financial district, the "hundred per cent location" keep their clout by performing so-called "central place functions." They aren't about to give up those functions to OUT THERE.

That's what "Downtown Days" are all about…bringing people back from OUT THERE; part of the eternal struggle between those who've got power, and those on the outside. The struggle continues between so-called "Users" and "Exploiters," those who use OUT THERE for domestic or local purposes, and others who want it for speculation, exchange, development, profit.

In deciding who's in, who's out, we become deeply divided… rich versus poor, the power elite versus the powerless, homefolks versus strangers, urban versus non-urban. The last census identified seventy-five percent of us as "urban." That leaves twenty-five percent OUT THERE, in the minority.

But, neither INS nor OUTS can exist without the other…the center and OUT THERE are the yin and yang of existence…all in the same boat. It's everybody's boat, and it's badly in need of repairs. This is no time to be OUT TO LUNCH.

The Sacred Path

All great religions require a code of conduct, a catechism, a set of commands about where and how to put on your good behavior—how to act in sacred places.

I happened to play midwife to such a code, in Boston, at a meeting of the National Association of Olmsted Parks—designed by the great Frederick Law Olmsted. It was the birth of a Movement with a capital M. All that was missing was a Code of Conduct. So I wrote one. It goes like this:

"Go ye among the multitudes and preach this, the way of the Great Designer, so that all may share his handiwork forevermore.

Impose not thy foreign will upon this place. Seek ye its Spirit and all else will follow.

Look thou to the earth and trees for thy sustenance and bring them no harm.

Know ye that the earth it is good, and he who treats it well, he shall have his own reward. And from him who bringeth damage and great harm, all shall be taken away.

Make no undue noises unto the high heavens. Nor shall ye push and shove thy neighbor between a rock and a hard place. Carry thyself gently, and there shall be space for all.

Bring not into this place any arms of war. Nor shall ye form yourselves into phalanxes or warlike groups. For this is a place of peace, and peaceful shall ye remain.

Do this in remembrance of the great Place Maker, whose firm hand can make us free to enjoy his places forever...."

And if that's too theological for you, how about this:

Keep off the Grass
Stay on the Paths
Don't Litter
Talk to Strangers

No Weapons
Share the Way
Leave the Place Cleaner Than You Found It
Enjoy the Views
No Artificial Noisemakers
Treat This Place as Your Home

Control

AIRSPACE

There once was a time when English common law assured the owner of a piece of land, the ownership of which extended to the high heavens above and into the bowels, if not the very center, of Earth below. That geometric icosahedron gave landowners a sense of control. It linked mankind, the gods, and the Devil himself...and Earth became their battleground.

That was before planes, rockets, and satellites. Before the so-called "Death of God." Before the birth of legal abstractions called "flight paths" and "air routes."

From that moment on, AIRSPACE has never been the same. AIRSPACE has turned into a crafted webbing, invisible to the naked eye. Once fancy-free, the plaything of gods and poets, it's now stock-in-trade to the aviation industry...185,637 nautical miles of exclusive commercial air routes. Go upward a bit, and you're into NASA turf, where AIRSPACE is littered with debris from dead or exploded rockets.

If you thought the air above your backyard belonged to you, think again. You CAN go fly a kite or model plane—but not too high, not too close to an airport.

It may be "your" AIRSPACE, but there's no way outside of court (lots of luck!) that you can block the all-seeing eye of satellites or legally intercept the mighty flow of electronic signals. Look up and listen! AIRSPACE, once free for all, is now an international grab bag.

ARREST HOUSE

Could ARREST HOUSE really be the newest sign of the times now that HOMEPLACE has been remodeled into that modern substitute for overcrowded jails or prisons? The ARREST HOUSE of the 1990s can be any house. No sign visible from the street reveals its grip. No neighbors are visibly alerted to the fact that a convicted felon, rapist, mugger, or drug dealer has been moved indoors, a detainee, a parolee-in-residence. Nobody would know, from the outside, that the person in the house is linked electronically to police headquarters, where his every move can be tracked. Or that the detainee must report regularly by telephone to distant keepers who can scan his or her personal voiceprint by electronics down at headquarters.

Such an ARREST HOUSE has peculiar assets. It can be a rented, non-public dwelling in which to stash prisoners. Plain-and-simple, it does not require a construction bond issue. It has precedents, for already in the 1980s we began to get privately run jailhouses that operate under contracts in converted motels, sanitaria, or apartments.

ARREST HOUSE does not lack for other precedents. A one-time owner of the famous Longfellow House in Cambridge, Massachusetts, was Andrew Craigie. After he declared bankruptcy, a serious offense in those days, Craigie was confined for the rest of his life, except for Sundays when he had indemnity from arrest. It's a beautiful tourist attraction on historic Brattle Street today. Not a bad place, if you choose to spend your declining years in a genteel ARREST HOUSE.

BLOCKADE

There's talk and a plan around my hometown to BLOCK off a main street, in this case called "Third Street," to expand a convention center. This latest form of BLOCKADE has historic precedents. In the Civil War, the Union BLOCKADED Southern ports; cut them off from overseas help; and, in effect, starved the South of supplies. Advocates of this BLOCKADE can find examples in the U.S. Navy, which has BLOCKADED dozens of countries in war and peace to starve or subdue the enemy.

In this local case, the enemy is we, people who look at a street, especially a street that's been doing a street's job for 200 years, and naturally and logically conclude "It's MY street," and "Don't you pass it off to somebody else who's gonna convert it to a BLOCKADE!"

Our language offers us other ways to describe BLOCKADE. It's A BLOCKAGE, A BLOCK, A BARRIER, AN OBSTACLE, A STUMBLING BLOCK.

To BLOCK is to obstruct or interfere with, to prevent the normal functioning of, to limit the use of...in this case, a street that we've been using, and benefiting from, for over 200 years.

I know Third Street well. I've worked on Third Street, lived on Third Street, was arrested for speeding on Third Street, attended a tiny drinking club on Third Street, and most often use Third Street as my favored entrance into my still-accessible downtown.

I drive past the next-worst thing to a BLOCKADE...that slab-sided monstrosity called the "Commonwealth Convention Center," and view with some alarm its expansion to BLOCKADE Third Street, to become a STUMBLING BLOCK; an even larger, immovable device for giving us the runaround; for converting downtown into an obstacle course and citizens into BLOCKADE RUNNERS. That's NOT what a street is supposed to do!

The author's testimony, based on this essay, helped persuade the Louisville Board of Aldermen to keep Third Street open.

The Courthouse Door

The courthouse door is also known as: auction site, vantage point, the heart of the political system, stoop, doorway, podium, promontory, center-stage, photo opportunity, and inauguration platform. Sociologists call it a "behavior setting."

It's the place where, in the last century, household goods of bankrupt settlers were sold at auction. Today it's where a sheriff's deputy steps up and posts legal notices. Pretty tame stuff.

Only yesterday politics was the damndest at THE COURTHOUSE DOOR. Everything happened on the steps or at the door: swearings in and swearing at, hustle and bustle, electioneering, speech making, flag-waving, arm-twisting, bloody shirting, fistfighting, and/or riots.

Once in awhile there was a shootout or an assassination. Remember Bloody Monday election day in Louisville or the murder of General Denhart in Shelbyville, Kentucky? THE COURTHOUSE STEPS also did bloody duty as dueling grounds.

Now it's a photo opportunity. Standing at THE COURTHOUSE DOOR, photographers can encompass speechmakers; hangers-on; passers by; the mostly peaceful picketers; that ubiquitous nonentity, the bystander; and in the background, traffic jam. On a dull news day, it seems to be the only game in town.

In the litigious 1960s, THE COURTHOUSE DOOR became a favorite locale for TV photographers to encourage protesters to "get a little action going." Sometimes following such advice, there ensued a modest but photogenic fracas. Later, in unfriendly courtrooms, this would be described as "inciting to riot."

In peaceful times, things are quiet if not dull here. But in times of trouble, we can expect the action to return to its old haunt— THE COURTHOUSE DOOR.

Flight Path

If you ever flew an old-time FLIGHT PATH, you know it hugged the ground and dodged tall trees. Once upon such a time, be-goggled pilots in open cockpits maintained a close visual contact with Mother Earth, ever ready for landing on her not-so-receptive bosom. Stunt flyers and barnstormers took all the Great Outdoors as their FLIGHT PATH.

But no longer. Now in middle age, FLIGHT PATH has grown rigid and prescribed; it's corseted, cosseted, regulated airspace. Close to airports it gets converted into approach zones, part of an environmental impact area.

Up there in the sky is something called "airspace." It's the world's largest four-dimensional subdivision…parceled out into highways and superhighways, complete with aerial equivalents of underpasses, overpasses, access lanes, dangerous intersections, bottlenecks, detours, and morning and evening rush hours. These are three-deckers, stacked up to 45,000 feet.

The New York TRACON (Terminal Radar Approach Control) on Long Island had 150 controllers in 1988 monitoring nearly two million flights a year through FLIGHT PATHS above four states. In 1992, New York TRACON was expected to handle 3,400 planes per hour.

You can't buy or sell a FLIGHT PATH eight miles wide and a thousand feet high at your local real estate office. You go through Washington lawyers and layers of congressmen.

Far above all this, the myriad FLIGHT PATHS of orbiting satellites go their not-so-merry way, some with military payloads, even into the era of post-Glasnost.

To all you travelers in the Great Out There, I commend the famous words of a Southern small-town flight controller, having erroneously instructed two pilots to land directly toward one another, head-on: "Y'ALL BE CAREFUL, NOW!"

Flood Hazard

I stood here, making these notes, in the place few people call by
its right name, "the floodway," also known as "The Ohio River
Valley," alongside that part of the floodway known as "The River
Road." All around me are BOTTOMS, land at the bottom of the
flood when it becomes a floodway, which also remind us that the
so-called "hundred-year flood" comes more often than it used to.
Here, by the road, stands a triangular blue sign. It says:
> FLOOD HAZARD AREA
> Base area elevation is
> approximately 13 feet above ground.
> For further information call Metropolitan-
> Sewer District or Division of Water

And the sign gives the telephone numbers to call.

Somebody wrote an angry, local letter to the editor complaining
about the government spending money for such a warning sign.
Are there folks so dumb or blind, or who just don't give a damn,
living and investing in the floodway? Have they been assured by
some duplicitous real-estate salesman that "Nobody around here
remembers any floods"?

Is some kind of community amnesia at work covering up the
fact that in 1937 our hometown was devastated by the so-called
"record flood"? And that a flood in 1964 covered hundreds of acres
of subdivisions that were maneuvered into place, defying the
regulations of the local planning commission?

You can travel a few miles up- or down-river and see what
is called an "urbanized area" with hundreds of houses and
businesses built OUTside the floodwalls and levees, right smack in
the floodway.

Shouldn't that little blue sign be changed to read "Future
Disaster Area"?

Flood Level

We had four inches of rain in forty minutes over my watershed the other day. That was an all-time record for my little trickle of a burble of a little, tiny stream. Four inches of rain in forty minutes overran the streets, the street drains, the alleys, and many yards. It picked up the gravel in one alley and deposited it along with mud on the streets. It topped my little dam and footbridges by a foot and left a foot of mud on the doorstep of my small springhouse.

Can you imagine, even after seeing it on television, what that seven-inch rainfall above Dubuque, Iowa, could do around here—just seven inches of it, all by itself?

Can you imagine what seven inches of rain in major parts of the Ohio River watershed would do? What it would be like—what it someday may be like—to have the kind of rainfall above our river city that they've had above another river city, St. Louis, Missouri?

The other day I went out and photographed the FLOOD LEVEL sign put up by the Corps of Engineers on roads along our great, placid, just-rolling-along Ohio River. I asked myself: what would happen in the floodway here with a Mississippi River type flood they're having there?

What would happen is that our floodway, a large slice of my county and yours, on both sides of the Ohio River, would take over its natural function of being a floodway. Homebuilders may convert it to valuable real estate, but it's basically floodway. People who build or buy homes flooded in the floodway would demand the government "do something" to bail them out of a predicament of their own choosing.

If you're among those thousands who choose to live in the floodway, look to the Mississippi flood and ask: Am I prepared to have it happen here?

Rising Tide

Millions of us—back here—are learning the language of floods—out there—on the Missouri and Mississippi Rivers.

Sloshing around in record floods this month, folks are forced to look at farms, towns, and highways and see places that now must be called by their real name—floodways. This comes hard to folks accustomed to looking at what they called "prime farmland, class A production sites for corn and soybeans." All now under water.

Floods penetrate language as well as landscape. Business is "down to a trickle" around the floodways. Rivers take on human attributes when the Associated Press writes of the "usually mild-mannered Raccoon River" now out of its banks. Floods, we are told, will be followed by a heavy flow of paperwork.

Meanwhile, there's a "RISING TIDE of concern" in Florida over the future of the Everglades. And if that weren't enough, there's a "RISING TIDE of takeovers" on Wall Street.

Headlines tell us that "Flood Costs Overflow the Estimates," and "the spillover effects" will be higher food prices. The "ripple effect" works overtime in the media. There are "fiscal floods of red ink" over the Midwest.

The Big River (Mississippi) not only is out of its banks, but as the Associated Press put it, "is pretty much in the driver's seat." And if all that weren't enough, "Riverboats open the floodgates," says one of my favorite columnists speaking of gambling boats proposed on the Ohio River. Once floods penetrate language, as well as landscape, there's no escape from the RISING TIDE. In those famous words that accompanied the 1937 flood in Louisville: "Send a Boat!"

SIZING UP

So you thought football field was the place for Saturday showdowns, first downs, touchdowns, comedowns and putdowns? Think again and listen to what happens to Saturday's lingo when it graduates from the sports pages.

Football field is proliferating to become our national unit measurement of size. Don't ask how. Just consider: Cincinnati's airport is expanding. The contractors dug up a prehistoric camp, some 3,000 years old. And how big was the camp? "About two football fields long," according to the *Cincinnati Enquirer*.

In the town of Napa, California, an eight-million-dollar house was destroyed by an explosion. How big was the explosion? It was heard miles away. And how big was the house? The size of a football field.

Near Juneau, Alaska, the second-largest glacier in North America is melting. It throws off icebergs large enough to threaten ships. And how big is that? As long as five football fields.

A man in Riverside, California, wrote us of the discovery of a giant Armillaria bulbosa mushroom. They grow in one triangular area, and all carry the same genetic fingerprint, identifying them as coming from a single plant. And how big is that single plant? More than five football fields in size.

The New Yorker Magazine reminds us that an international flower auction in Alsmeer, Holland, was held in a building twelve times the size of a football field.

My favorite originates from Erma Bombeck, the columnist, who said, "With all the flap about nutrition, Americans devoured seventy-one football fields of pizza a day last year."

Which gets us across the goal line of that new American one-hundred-yard yardstick, football field.

The Furrow

It started out small, primitive, scratchy. A miserable thing it was, the first FURROW, that first hole in the ground that became a slice in the ground for planting a food crop. Maybe as early as 3,000 BC the first FURROWS turned up in Egypt—some say in Mesopotamia.

Since then, FURROWS have come a fur-piece, as they say out on the Back Forty. Most of our food depends on mechanical energy applied to a blade, a knife, a plow, a disk, or a scoop drawn across the ground in a continuous, but not necessarily straight line.

That first, forcible entry prized open the earth's surface to make a predictable crop. And from the FURROW came surpluses of wheat to be stored away, carried off, fought over, traded, sold, and shipped. The shores of the Mediterranean Sea became the Roman Empire's breadbasket.

And, like anything so important, THE FURROW became standardized—by an English king, Edward the first—around the year 1300. He set the standard English plowing strip as one FURROW long—forty rods, 220 yards. Today we call it "The Furlong."

When the thoroughbred horses go to the post on Kentucky Derby Day, when they go the distance to the finish line, that distance is measured on King Edward's terms—in furlongs. That's quite a distance from Egypt and Mesopotamia where the race for food and the expansion of the human race started with a FURROW in the ground. It's come all the way to Churchill Downs, where the Run for the Roses takes place every first Saturday in May.

Holdouts

Its proper name is HOLDOUT. Not the verb TO HOLD OUT, but the noun HOLDOUT. It's that old farmhouse with a new shopping center alongside. It's that stubborn little Mom-and-Pop grocery store, overshadowed by the new skyscraper next door. HOLDOUT! It's that cattle rancher who fights off the new National Park proposed to cover his valley. HOLDOUT!

It's hard to imagine any community without HOLDOUTS, without some interruptions in the steady march of solid building blocks over house and farm and hill and dale. If we favor progress over history, if we prefer the newfangled to the old-fashioned, we sneer at the word HOLDOUT. We talk about that stubborn stick-in-the-mud landowner who stands in the way of progress by refusing to sell out. But if we prefer to be surrounded by a familiar framework, then we support our local historical HOLDOUTS and raise hell with anybody wanting to knock them down.

When there's a depression going on, HOLDOUTS get little attention. Everything's ON HOLD. But come the next building boom, city hall drips with solicitude for developers who promise to clear out the HOLDOUTS built by the city. Building inspectors come under pressure to look the other way while HOLDOUTS decay, hoping the neighbors will gang up against those old eyesores, the HOLDOUTS.

It's a mixed bag out there: carpetbaggers and developers pushing and shoving to get rid of HOLDOUTS versus local folks anxious to hold out against change. The disputes that tear communities apart are those that come when all this developmental hugger-mugger is accomplished in secret.

LULU

LULU is the name, politics is the game, and the name of the game is to bash, prevent, or even outlaw LULUS. For LULU, in case you need be reminded, stands for "Locally Unwanted Land Use." LULU.

In your neighborhood a duplex might be a LULU. Or a junkyard, housing for the elderly, a golf course subdivision, or a highway interchange.

For a nation populated by a hundred-million homeowners with millions more arriving every year, one person's LULU is another person's asset.

LULU came into vogue and into the language in the 1980s, chiefly among homeowners who flocked to zoning hearings to protest LULUS. (LULUS are also known as NIMBYS, which stands for "Not In My Back Yard.")

What gives LULUS the power to upset, to excite, to agitate, are the homeowners' expectations—against all evidence—that once they move into a neighborhood, the world will stop dead in its tracks. No additional neighbors, no additional traffic. The last one in wants to be the last one let in. Close the gate! Bar the door!

But those who close gates and bar doors forget there's no neighborhood without community, and no community can survive if its members don't learn to live with differences... whether they be lulus, nimbys, or just strangers.

Queue

The QUEUE. That's Q-U-E-U-E. If there's a line, most people believe there's something worth waiting for at the end of it. Every day, more of us turn into schedule-keepers, and standing-in-liners. QUEUING up consumes five years of the average American lifetime according to Priority Management of Pittsburgh. If each of us spends a daily QUEUE-time of thirty minutes, that's thirty-seven billion hours stuck in line per year.

How do we cope? People in QUEUES pull out Walkman radios, portable TVs, or paperback books. A few strike up conversation. Up alongside the QUEUE come jugglers, sidewalk entertainers, beggars, political hand-outers, and volunteers of every kind.

At stoplights and outside bridges and tunnels, hawkers peddle flowers and holiday stuff to uptight drivers all QUEUED up. In shops you get shouldered into the checkout line by cigarette and candy machines and magazine racks.

The willingness of the English to QUEUE up politely is evidence of "a discipline by which an historically aggressive people reminded themselves that they were civilized." But QUEUING up also offers countless chances to get out of line. Remember when the gasoline shortages in 1973 caused long lines at gas stations? Some customers fought, some offered cash or sex for a place in line.

Society's ability, or refusal, to wait in line is a measure not only of its civility, but its fitness for a future life of stop-and-go. Be prepared for long waits....

SPHERES OF INFLUENCE

Every anniversary of President John Kennedy's assassination
brings up the old conspiracy theories all over again. While that
one has been pretty well shot down, if you want more exposure to
paranoia, just bring up the matter of SPHERES OF INFLUENCE.

When I took my college course in European history, a SPHERE
OF INFLUENCE was strictly geographic. It was the place where
the British Navy held the British Empire together across the
Mediterranean and the Indian Ocean.

But the other day I happened into a discussion of SPHERES OF
INFLUENCE, and believe you me, it moved the old-fashioned
geographic SPHERE OF INFLUENCE out of geography books.

So! You thought the North American Free Trade Agreement
got through congress by the usual horse-trading of votes among
White House lobbyists and senators and congressmen to improve
the American economy? WRONG. According to conspiratorial
theory it was a dark conspiracy among a secret cabal—"them"—
expanding their SPHERE OF INFLUENCE to weaken the United States.

So! You think the ascendancy of women into politics reflects
the rising number of women who work and vote? WRONG.
According to conspiracy theory expressed to me by a couple of
angry males, it's the work of THEM, a dark and sinister cabal of
women expanding their SPHERE OF INFLUENCE—assisted by the
wife of the president!

Ask who THEY are. What you get is the runaround. Vague
allegations, veiled innuendo rising to a crescendo of..."well you
know who THEY are!"

It's a familiar story. In troubled times, people are suckers for
conspiracy theory. They round up the usual suspects and get
trapped by talk of secret SPHERES OF INFLUENCE. Don't let it
happen to you.

State Line

If any of you have asked why in the world those Bosnians keep on fighting in the Balkans, take another look at our own geography in this valley of the great Ohio River.

The way some people talk on either side of that river, you'd think this boundary between Kentucky and Indiana were as impermeable as those old, nationalistic borders in Central Europe.

It's true Kentuckians and Hoosiers are not shooting each other. But long ago, Louisville took down the welcome sign that said "Gateway to the South" on the Clark Memorial Bridge.

So the other day I made some test approaches to Louisville from the north. I could find nothing...no prominent signs on the Louisville skyline to welcome travelers, commuters, or curiosity-seekers from across the river.

Mapmakers are still notoriously reluctant to show the Other Side in significant detail on "our maps."

Not long ago I was party to a discussion among book writers from both sides of the Ohio River about identifying ourselves as a "Kentuckiana" group—a bit of wordplay to embrace both sides of this metropolitan region. It was attacked with some anger by a Kentuckian who wanted nothing to do with a hybrid called "Kentuckiana."

When some Louisvillians talk about the inevitable new bridges to connect Indiana and Kentucky, it's as though their hometown were to be invaded by foreign traffic. Fortunately, the majority appears to support one or more new bridges.

But until both sides of that old boundary line between North and South recognize how much we depend upon each other for transactions, goods, services, and human contact, we'll still be confronting these little bloodless reminders of a long-gone, bloody Civil War.

At Large

At Large

While many Americans have been looking the other way, a new place has been injected into their landscape. It's ill-fit; it barely reaches everyday language, and it hangs out on the fringes of academia. Like other new phenomena, it gets called up by familiar words and phrases. But what best fits is the expression "AT LARGE."

AT LARGE is a changing neighborhood. People use the phrase AT LARGE loosely to describe that risky realm where escaped criminals and runaway kids are known to be AT LARGE. This specific sense of the word is now, I think, moving aside to allow for expanded meanings to creep in.

In its new venue, AT LARGE is a place of loose attachments. AT LARGE there are no strings. It offers footloose and up-anchored freedom. AT LARGE is a place that invites high jinks, free spirits, freestanding personalities and freewheeling movement. It's freelancers' heaven on earth.

If you're an ambassador AT LARGE, you're not stuck with one piece of geography; the world is your oyster, or so you may think. If you're a delegate AT LARGE, you've got a chance to define your own duties, all by yourself.

AT LARGE seems to exist free for the taking, a place to take liberty, if not to spend your leave. But it's a risky, chancy world, all by yourself, way out there, AT LARGE. And to be all things to all people is no simple assignment. Sometimes being AT LARGE may be enroute to THE EXIT.

My advice would be: next time you're asked to DO or BE anything or anybody AT LARGE, get it in writing well ahead of time.

BACK

Emergencies, such as a snow emergency caused by a sudden sixteen inches of snow, and a cold wave across Middle America, have a way of separating the sheep from the goats, the four-wheelers from the stuck-in-the-snow, those who cope from those who can't, and especially THE FRONT from THE BACK.

All of a sudden THE BACK turned into THE BOONDOCKS, if not into THE GREAT BEYOND. Anything out in the BACKYARD or on a BACK ROAD was out of reach, stuck in THE STICKS.

With no warning except that sudden silence of falling snow, thousands of families discovered they were living on, although nobody told them, a BACK STREET, SIDE STREET, SECONDARY ROAD or, worst of all, a BACK ROAD. If they wanted OUT, they had to walk OUT, dig OUT, or wait it OUT.

Overnight, thousands of streets, roads, trails, alleys, access ramps—even the great interstates—were converted to THE OUTBACK, inaccessible, off the beaten path, off the map, out of the running.

Millions of families found themselves no longer UP FRONT, deprived of that thing most folks take for granted in this mobility-driven society—INSTANT ACCESS.

Door-to-door deliveries? Forget it. Do the Ford and Toyota assembly plants count on just-in-time deliveries? Shut 'em down. A quick run across town? No way.

Suddenly, snowbound families found themselves second-class citizens. No authority, except nature itself, gave the first orders: STAY BACK, INDOORS, KEEP BACK, GET BACK, GO BACK, BACK OFF, LIE BACK—but don't BACK UP if you don't have chains or four-wheel drive.

And don't get your BACK up about it. Pitch in and help if you can. Those are the lessons when nature itself gets its BACK up.

Sprawl

When the federal interstate highway program was let loose after 1954, it was as though millions of cheap acres of farmland were being loaded onto flatcars and dumped right next door to millions of American customers in the cities.

There was no turning back the tide. By the 1970s new job creation was distinctly suburban.

THE BURBS. That's the short name for it, that vast collection of SUBURBIAS, OUTSKIRTS, EXURBS, YUPPIE ENCLAVES, and other COMMUTER DESTINATIONS...all created by cheap gasoline protected by a war in the Arabian Gulf, and cheap mortgages back home.

On their own inner-directed terms, THE BURBS are a success. They succeeded on the American landscape by putting cheap distance between where people work and where they sleep. In the ideal BURB, distance is everything.

It was to protect the Gulf oil supplies so as to keep this distance cheap that the U.S. waged war on Iraq in 1992. Few man-made places can make that boast.

So what other man-made place has picked up a majority of the American population in three generations? THE BURBS became the seat of geographic power. Without THE BURBS, cities would shrivel, and would-be presidents would lose elections. Without commuters from THE BURBS, workstations would go empty, employers would go broke, and industries that depend on oil would shrink.

The key to all this is distance. People who move to THE BURBS bought distance from neighbors. They pay for it with cheap mortgages, single-family zoning, deed restrictions, big lots, fences, and shrubbery. They keep their distance by regulating what leaps across it: strangers, noise, outdoor cooking smells, trash burning, or trailers, campers, or trucks. Few cocks to crow or bulls to bellow in THE BURBS.

What folks out there want are city services—at a cut rate. Meanwhile, the city-left-behind tries to invent new forms of "citizenship" that can overcome the distance between DOWNTOWN and THE BURBS. To find meeting grounds is going to take a steady struggle.

But then, recall that first whiff of The Limits—the Arab oil embargo of 1974. Millions of Americans found themselves stuck in long queues waiting for scarce gasoline. Its price per gallon tripled.

Thus began the long struggle, still under way, to strip THE BURBS and their commuting routes of gas-guzzling cars and trucks. Here began federal programs to improve mass transit among THE BURBS and their parent DOWNTOWNS—often thwarted by oil lobbyists in and around congress.

Meanwhile, the city BACK THERE began its bumpy efforts to survive on a shrinking tax base. It tried to overcome distance by an occupational tax on commuters where they worked. It struggled to form metropolitan governments, coalitions, treaties, and compacts.

The struggle goes on. The infatuation with suburban life has yet to meet the crises yet to come.

The Circle

I've been circling around this subject, looking for an opening, trying to find a gap so I could dash through to the heart of the matter.

The object I've been circling is the map of my city. Most maps show the Great Circle Route of the future, the interstate circular highway around your metropolis or mine.

The first thing you notice about these circles, whether you see them on the map or meet them on the ground, are the gaps. Several gaps. Unbuilt gaps. Two of them interstate gaps; one gap so long it may be politically unbuildable for a long time to come.

Of course, people who fight traffic to get around the gaps want to close them, and that's partly what the current debate over bridge locations is about.

But that's not ALL it's about. There's magic in the air. We speak of THE MAGIC CIRCLES. Old folk tales remind us of the MAGIC RING of mushrooms in the woods. To belong to THE INNER CIRCLE carries prestige; to sit in THE DRESS CIRCLE carries a pricey tag; to be in THE FAMILY CIRCLE brings comfort; to get to THE WINNER'S CIRCLE at Churchill Downs can cost you, and get you, millions of bucks.

Which brings us back to the gaps in the interstate. It's not just a line on the map. It's a circle and it carries all the magic that's hung around circles for thousands of years. And our discontent will be with us until, for better or for worse, we fill the gaps, complete the ring, close the magic circle, and get on with metropolitan life.

EARSHOT

Noise, as distinct from sound, is something other people make, and we dislike. If it's strange, uninvited, and within EARSHOT, we object.

"Since noise was recognized as a problem in Britain in the early 1960s, it has been treated as a pollutant. But noise is not like other pollutants." We can't always predict its effects.

The way we perceive noise is quite personal and culturally determined. You golfers may recall, in a story by P.G. Wodehouse, the nervous golfer who, when trying to putt, complained about "the roar of butterflies." I myself once felt impelled to write a code of conduct for public parks designed by Frederick Law Olmsted. And I admonished everybody within EARSHOT, "No artificial noisemakers."

The noise of aircraft has become our most invasive domestic racket. Many airport authorities are buying out or soundproofing the houses or offices of neighbors within close EARSHOT.

But noise is also a sign of life. In Brazil, to say that a town is movimentado, that is, bustling, thus noisy, is a compliment indeed. The idea that noise is bad and quiet is good runs counter to the notion that activity (life) is good and inactivity (death) is bad.

Whether loud music of rock and roll and punk rock positively damages human hearing is no longer a matter for debate. But adult antagonism toward "that goddamn noise," whether human or otherwise, also usually expresses social disapproval of the source when it comes within EARSHOT.

SILENCE

City people get accustomed to noise, so that when they pick up and go out deeeeep into REAL COUNTRY, far beyond the BACK FORTY, well into THE BOONDOCKS, surrounded by THE OUTBACK, out in that extended territory called "OUT THERE," they are seized by the SILENCES, dumfounded, if not thunderstruck, to be within earshot of absolutely NO artificial noisemakers whatever.

Did you notice, in that last sentence, I used "SILENCE" in the plural—SILENCES? Pretty soon you learn to distinguish between SILENCES—SILENCE at dawn, SILENCE at midnight, frightening SILENCE, reassuring SILENCE.

But most of all, you're into absolutely no noise, no-how. No trucks on the interstate, no hot-rodders on the boulevard, no lawnmowers next door, no leaf blowers, no boom boxes. Just the absence of what, to some people, city life is all about; that is, somebody else's noise. To be in a city is to live with noise—background noise, pervasive noise, ambient noise.

But hold on. There's this metropolitan county that has had the audacity, if not temerity, not to mention the bravado, to pass a new ordinance against those needless, heedless, bad-neighborly noisemakers that invade that personal place called "earshot"—hot-rodders with no mufflers (already illegal), stereo boom boxes—on four wheels or on two feet. I've been told that often the key is whether the noise constitutes a nuisance when far away from its source.

In other words, to keep that place called "earshot" pleasurable, be sure it's measurable.

LEAF PEEPERS

The production line has done its work. The product is packaged, on display, in the marketplace. It's a HIT. Photographers, the moment they see it, get itchy trigger fingers. Jaundiced journalists drop their objectivity and spread-eagle their prose.

I'm talking about "fall color country," also known as "fall foliage country." It's the essence of contrived semi-reality…"countryside" reconstituted; merchandisable; panoramic; fully furnished with Picturesque—capital "P"—white-steepled villages; hillsides glowing, golden, gleaming.

But maybe you forget? Once upon a time, fall color country did not yet exist as a mass-produced generic place. It was old New England, carved off from the Indians, settled in time for Thanksgiving.

But today, it's been converted to "cultural artifact," a coming attraction, to be touristicated, visitated, photographed, hyped-up, paid for. All credit cards accepted.

Not only in New England. From coast to coast it generates traffic jams and a hundred-million dollars a year. A boat skipper offers Fall Foliage Tours on the Tennessee River out of Chattanooga. In the Rockies, the golden aspens quiver and quake on cue.

Merchants depend on it, like Christmas shopping, to make their season. Networks of LEAF PEEPERS follow the colors day by day. Are we in time for peak color?

But soon enough, death creeps in, bright colors peak and fade away. And it's check-out time at the newly restored historic gristmill, time to say farewell to fall color country.

WITHIN RANGE

GUNSHOT, according to one definition, is the sound you hear when a gun goes off. But that's not the whole story. Consider the phrase "WITHIN GUNSHOT." That diverts our attention from the noise of the shot to the location of the gun and the shooter. How far are we from the gun barrel? Are we WITHIN RANGE?

Now THAT covers a huge territory. In private hands in the United States, there are believed to be some two-hundred-million guns. Gun sales have been running around four to five million per year, including about two-million handguns. Gun shooting, the activity itself, is claiming about a thousand lives each year. For people who are black and between the ages 15 to 19, getting shot while WITHIN RANGE is now the leading cause of death in the United States.

Now, if I may coin a phrase, "within handgunshot" is a killing ground with a radius of roughly 200 feet, depending on the type of gun and the aim of the shooter. But a handgun might carry further than 200 feet, mightn't it? Conservatively calculated, the range of a handgun covers about two and a half acres. This suggests that another five-million acres of the United States come WITHIN RANGE of new weapons every year.

This also suggests that at this rate, most metropolitan residents of the United States, except for Alaskans and other remote boondockers, will soon be WITHIN RANGE of somebody with a gun.

We've come a long way since 1990, when most of us were thought to be within inter-ballistic-missile-type range of the Russians. Now we're at peace with Russia and WITHIN RANGE has moved closer to home.

Y'all be careful now!

GUNSHOT

GUNSHOT is spelled G-U-N-S-H-O-T, and if you take it the way I take it, it's a place, not just the sound you hear when a gun goes off. And a dangerous place to be. Consider the expression "within GUNSHOT." It locates you, the gun, and the shooter. In proximity. The question is: Where are you and where is the shooter AT? As they ask in court: "Were you within GUNSHOT?"

Good question when deer season is here, depending on where you are right now.

The real question is: Is your house located within GUNSHOT of a hedgerow, woodlot, deer stand, deer woods, or even a thicket? If you're NOT a hunter, do you dare go outdoors?

In scores of states, including Kentucky, the deer population is expanding, getting out of hand, but not out of GUNSHOT. Meanwhile, the human population in suburbia spreads itself out, putting itself in harm's way, within GUNSHOT of the growing host of hunters and their increasingly high-powered rifles.

It's a high-velocity mixture. You've heard the horror story of Karen Wood, the thirty-seven-year-old mother of twins "shot dead in her own woodsy backyard in the brand-new suburbs of Bangor, Maine."[1] The hunter who shot her—he mistook her white mitten for the white tail of a deer—was arrested for manslaughter and acquitted: the lady was NOT wearing the standard blaze orange in hunting season.

Terrible stuff, reminding us again that GUNSHOT is not just a condition, but a place as dangerous as your own outer-suburban backyard or back forty in hunting season.

1: Michael Spected, "Riflefire in the New Suburbia: Whose Woods? Hunter vs. Homeowner", *New York Times*, November 29, 1992.

Inauguration Route

Welcome to INAUGURATION ROUTE, the Mecca of millions of hero-worshippers. Now that President Clinton has been packaged for posterity, now that the parade is over, now that…isn't it time to take a second look at INAUGURATION ROUTE? At what's behind that vivid scenery?

There's the place we conduct the peak ceremony of the civil religion of the United States. We watch the new President, master of the religious ritual, getting sworn in—"So Help Me God!" He's the latest of the revered and not-so-revered, holy and not-so-holy, male occupants of the highest office in Washington.

Since the United States set itself free from official state religions, we've gradually wrapped around the presidential office the trappings of a civil religion. We pray to many gods to watch over the President. We capitalize the title with a capital "P." We convert the American flag into a sacred object. We bring up the chief justice, the man in the long, black robe, to swear the President into office. The justices preside as high priests, to proclaim dogma and holy writ as it appears, somewhat dimly, in the Constitution.

You can say, as the noted geographer Wilbur Zelinski has said, that "Nationalistic monuments fulfill the role of wayside shrines." The secret service's budget costs taxpayers over a million dollars a day to serve and protect this holy office and the sacred path between The Capitol and The White House.

Perhaps as many as fifty million of us, like Mohammedans to Mecca, pilgrimage every year to such national shrines as the Washington Monument, Lincoln Memorial, and National Parks. And yet, since the bicentennial year of 1976, pilgrimages to most of these shrines have fallen off. Is that a sign that the civil religion itself grows weaker?

The Light—After The Bomb

In this New Year, now that THE BOMB is no longer an everyday presence; now that global extinction, as a clear and present danger, has passed from the scene; now that atomic warfare between America and the USSR is no longer a presence in everyday life; at long last it is possible for each of us to take a new look around at our place in the world. Looking around no longer requires us to think about extinction and the end of the earth.

That's not a bad way to start the New Year, now is it? At long last, after a generation of the Cold War, the chances are we will still be here and more or less in place. Chances are the places we hold dear to our hearts—house and home, turf and territory, the daily round, home place and workplace—will still be here tomorrow, where we want them and expect them to be. They will not disappear.

Without THE BOMB as a prospect, the world, almost all of a sudden, has begun to look more stable. Even the turmoil in Bosnia and Somalia assumed its more logical and limited place in the world.

Now we can feel the cold, wintry wind from Siberia without thinking how easily we could become downwind of an atomic explosion. We can look at the wintry sun and not wonder if its soft rays will disappear in a dusty holocaust of radioactivity.

And so, for this New Year, we are set free—free at last!—to live in a world not lit by the flash of THE BOMB, living in a land that is alight with new hope for peace in our time. And that is not at all a bad place to be.

PATCHES

There was this young woman from Natchez
Whose clothing was covered with PATCHES
When comments arose
On the state of her clothes
She drawled "When ah itches ah scratches."

There are, of course, other kinds of PATCHES...BRIAR PATCH, that obscure refuge frequented by unforgettable Br'er Rabbit in Southern folk tales by Joel Chandler Harris. There's DOGPATCH, the haunt of Li'l Abner and the comic strip Yokums. Remember the fad for Cabbage PATCH Dolls that grew out of a Louisville place immortalized in the story "Mrs. Wiggs of the Cabbage PATCH"?

Moving up-scale, there's MELLON PATCH, used to describe Pittsburgh, since 1970 a town influenced, then dominated by the wealthy family of Mellons—spelled with two "L"s.

Do you recall, back early in the George W. Bush administration, how much was made of the OIL PATCH? That was the just-folksy title that Texas oil drillers and suppliers used to downplay their wealth and presidential connection.

PATCH has come a long way from cabbages, Br'er Rabbit, and melons. It's come through the language of ecology, past oil fields, and into cities.

Now PATCHES are everywhere, irregular gatherings of collective human energy into special locations. They gather, often anonymous and by accident, in tent cities after disasters, becoming instant neighborhoods; old blocks burned to the ground, rebuilt anew; old fairgrounds converted to apartments; exhausted oil fields segue into warehousing; old warehouse districts get boutiqued until boutiques run out of fashion.

Come to think of it, cities are made of PATCHES, some with names, some buried in PATCHwork, overlooked.

POCKET

Has somebody got you "in their POCKET?" Are you broke and, as they say, "out of POCKET"? Do you live in a "POCKET of unemployment"?

POCKET is one of those places that doesn't exist in nature, but we language-using folks have been trying to fill the vacuum ever since we put language to work.

The key thing about a place called a "POCKET" is that it's isolated, limited, restricted. It's out of sight, out of mind. It's probably a leftover, overlooked. It's a "POCKET of resistance" left behind, in ignominious isolation, by victorious troops. Or a dead end into which you've been propelled against your wishes. Or a POCKET of poverty abandoned or never even touched by prosperity.

General usage, with its high rank and prestige, suggests POCKET is an isolated condition, even an oddity. The inference is loud and clear: POCKET is a phenomenon not in the mainstream.

But watch it, there. A POCKET can often be a telltale indicator of a widespread condition. You get enough local "POCKETS of unemployment" and you've got unemployment. A "POCKET of pus" can indicate a spreading infection.

It often turns out that POCKETS are handy dumping grounds for things we don't want to know about or wish to push aside.

While a watch POCKET may be a place to PUT a watch, most POCKETS turn out to be places to watch. So as you go through your day, keep your eyes peeled for POCKETS.

Stink Zones

The other day, someWHERE, someHOW, someBODY, by doing the wrong thing or NOT doing the right thing, let loose a terrible stinky-stench across town. Four miles away, I caught a strong whiff of it. Something in the air smelled fishy, rotten, pungent, nasty—that is, it STUNK! It came from a chemical plant that makes, of all innocent causes of a stink, feed supplement for animals.

The next morning my friendly local newspaper referred, in somewhat prissy fashion, I thought, to "The Odor." But the following day, the paper did get down to brass tacks, down to earth, down in the gutter, and printed the "S" word: S-T-I-N-K.

But nowhere in all the media coverage could I find any word to describe that several square miles of my city that had been stunk up.

It was not enough to say, "I was 'downwinded.'" And to say, "My house is in the STINK ZONE" sounds somewhat contrived, made up, doesn't it?

Suddenly I recalled that wonderfully useful prefix, that front-end loader of meaning, spelled "B-E." As in words like BEsmogged, BEsmirched, BEsplattered, BEspoiled, BEdrizzled, BEdraggled—all good old English words that suggest that we've been overcome, overwhelmed, overtaken by forces outside ourselves.

But in all such word-mongering, something was still missing. Shouldn't there be a word for A PLACE where folks have been subjected, against their wishes, to a STINK? Their air has been BEFOULED (there's a good BE-word) They feel BELEAGUERED, BEFLUSTERED.

Now we're getting close. Let's say "They have been BESTUNK; their neighborhood has become A BESTUNK ZONE."

If you can think of a better (or worse) term for any place subjected to unwelcome STINK, feel free to use it.

STUD

The next time you see a colorful place-name in a headline, the key question to ask is: Does that place actually show up in the article itself? Is there a THERE there?

Sometimes, as Gertrude Stein once said in a put-down of her hometown, Oakland, California, "When you get there, there's no THERE there."

Take the expression "going to STUD," which, in a manner of speaking, resembles "going to seed." The other day, in a well-known newspaper, it was trotted out to describe a local congressman who's not going to run again. He's out of the race, out of the running, no longer in the field, off the track, out of competition. Or, as the headline said, "going to STUD."

Nowhere in that political news column itself did the word "STUD" show up. It was purely an interjection by the headline writer who picked up on other horseracing terms from the column and added his key headline word, "STUD."

Time was when STUD couldn't get through the gate to polite society. It ALWAYS referred to a particular place, generally a STUD farm, where thoroughbred stallions stood at STUD, ready to "service" (as it was round-aboutly expressed) a mare to produce a foal, a colt, and a possible winner of the Kentucky Derby.

But now STUD has moved into wider circulation to describe a congressman going to STUD when all it means in his most innocent of worlds is "not running for congress again."

This clearly has nothing to do with the sexual activity of a member of the U.S. House of Representatives. It has EVERYTHING to do with the mobile activity of language. What this means is: Watch those expressions as they come 'round the bend and head down the stretch, cross the finish line, and head back to the stables. The meaning may change as fast as the odds on the race.

The Water

I'm about to jump into DEEP WATER, talking about being UP THAT NASTY, DIRTY-WORD CREEK WITHOUT A PADDLE. And no doubt I'll be accused of having WATER ON THE BRAIN. But it does occur to me, and perhaps others, that we'd be UP THE CREEK, stuck with our everyday, indoor language, if we didn't reach out to The Great Outdoors where so many of our comparisons and similes and examples have their beginnings. Yet we are forever dragging these outdoor words indoors to do indoor work.

I don't need to remind you that our language would dry up and blow away if we quit borrowing expressions, most of them called "metaphors," from the outdoor world.

Say you're talking nonsense—most of us do sometimes, or even often. Somebody else is quick to say, "You're over your head," or "Don't muddy THE WATERS," or "You're out of your depth." If it's wintertime, you can be accused of "skating on thin ice."

If somebody jumps you too hard, you can always shrug and say, "Well, that's WATER over the dam," or give it a variation and say, "That's WATER under the bridge."

If the subject is too abstract, abstruse, if not impenetrable, you can, of course, fall back on the nautical expression and say, "It's unfathomable," and then try to switch channels, which, of course, might get you into still deeper WATER.

But now it's high summertime…time to make a splash, to make waves, to get in the swim. And you don't, my darling daughter, have to go near the WATER!

WATERSHED

What would political commentators do without WATER and WATERSHEDS? I mean, how would they tell how to "go with the FLOW"? How else could the columnist Kevin Phillips have handled the last election without calling it a "WATERSHED election"? What would happen to the Supreme Court if it could no longer render important WATERSHED decisions?

Do we have WATER on the brain? The answer clearly is YES. Our language has WATER on the brain, WATER over the dam, WATER under the bridge, and WATER penetrating everyday usage. WATER taking vigorous, metaphorical, leaps, making a splash, even up into dry territory, beyond the HIGH WATER MARK.

If a lawyer gets bogged down in fuzzy logic, you say, "He's in MURKY WATER." Or, stuck with a case he can't handle, "He's in DEEP WATER, OVER HIS HEAD." If a stockbroker adds phony value to a stock, he's WATERED it down, right?

There's no limit to our ability to grab good outdoor words and drag them kicking and screaming to do metaphorical duty indoors, far from their original source.

If a man's pants are too short, he's accused of wearing HIGH-WATER BRITCHES. If he puts on airs, he's said to be WALKING ON WATER. If he's exhausted, his energies, like the tides, are at LOW EBB. If the subject matter is too complicated, it's said to be UNFATHOMABLE—that's from the nautical measure of WATER depth, a fathom, which is six feet.

WATERS can even ascend into the intellectual reaches of Oxford University, for it was there the great English historian, Isaiah Berlin, said that, in reading an article by his compatriot, Lewis Namier, "One had the sensation, for which there is no substitute, of suddenly sailing in FIRST CLASS WATERS."[1]

And that's a good place to be...in FIRST CLASS WATERS, not AT SEA.

1: "Personal Impressions" by Isaiah Berlin, (Penguin 1980).